CALMING
THE BRAIN
THROUGH
MINDFULNESS
AND CHRISTIAN
MEDITATION

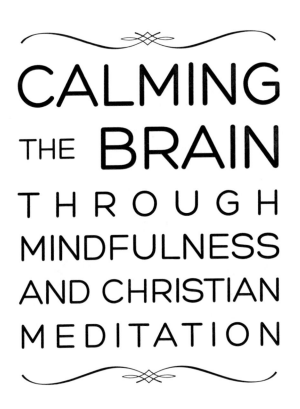

CALMING
THE BRAIN
THROUGH
MINDFULNESS
AND CHRISTIAN
MEDITATION

DR. MARK BEISCHEL

TATE PUBLISHING
AND ENTERPRISES, LLC

This book is designed to provide accurate and authoritative information with regard to the subject matter covered. This information is given with the understanding that neither the author nor Tate Publishing, LLC is engaged in rendering legal, professional advice. Since the details of your situation are fact dependent, you should additionally seek the services of a competent professional.

The opinions expressed by the author are not necessarily those of Tate Publishing, LLC.

Published by Tate Publishing & Enterprises, LLC
127 E. Trade Center Terrace | Mustang, Oklahoma 73064 USA
1.888.361.9473 | www.tatepublishing.com

Tate Publishing is committed to excellence in the publishing industry. The company reflects the philosophy established by the founders, based on Psalm 68:11,
"The Lord gave the word and great was the company of those who published it."

Book design copyright © 2016 by Tate Publishing, LLC. All rights reserved.
Cover design by Dante Rey Redido
Interior design by Mary Jean Archival

Published in the United States of America

ISBN: 978-1-68301-387-7
1. Body, Mind & Spirit / Mindfulness & Meditation
2. Self-Help / Self-Management / General
16.01.14

Contents

Preface

MANY OF MY PAST PATIENTS and other individuals I have known live very stressed lives, worrying about the future or feeling guilty about the past. Teasdale, Williams, and Segal (2014), in a recent training manual on mindfulness, quote a patient, "My problem was always lying awake at night brooding about what happened at work during the day and worrying about what was going to happen tomorrow." Individuals like this do not seem to have developed a resilient ego that is satisfied and content with the present activity and experience. As a result, they seem to be stuck in a very anxious state of mind. In this book, we are going to explain this phenomenon from attachment theory and recent brain research.

In medical settings, the brain is calmed by medications that may have serious side effects over time and could become addictive. I do not think that this is necessary and so suggest that there are "tried and true" means of calming down the anxious brain: mindfulness, prayer, and meditation. Herbert

Benson's (2010) research at Harvard University suggests that the brain can be relaxed through meditation, repetitive prayer, repetitive aerobic exercise, Eastern meditation, progressive muscle relaxation, playing or listening to music, and engaging in tasks requiring "mindless" repetitive movements. We will explore all these avenues as means of relaxing the brain. Finally we will suggest that praying the psalms in specific situations on a daily basis, as done by monks and religious people for many centuries, may be the appropriate way for those with Judo-Christian beliefs to quell the anxieties of life.

Louis Cozolino (2006) has made a compelling argument that the human brain is social by nature. Our brains have evolved over many millions of years into social organs that are being built over our life span through our experiences in human relationships, beginning with our first relationships with our mothers and fathers. This first attachment/ relationship sets the stage for all future relationships.

If we were fortunate enough to have the good grace of having parents who were responsive to our first cries, we begin believing that we are worth caring for and that parents will take care of our needs and threats no matter what comes in our small lives. As a result, whenever we have needs or threats, we scurry to our parents for protection and survival. This, of course, is the ethological attachment theory developed by John Bowlby (1962, 1982). He thought that the inclination to seek proximity to the attachment figure (mother or father) was a behavior system that evolved for the protection of the species. In this sense then, attachment is a normal and healthy characteristic that we use throughout the life span in order to survive. This dependency on others is not a sign of "immaturity" that needs to be outgrown (as some would say) but rather the result of evolution that should be celebrated rather than discarded over the life span. The American "spirit" of independence often presses us in another direction developmentally. The theology of the body of Christ suggests that we are one body (the church) connected by faith similar to the connections of neurons (as explained by Cozolino above).

In this book, we will come to understand that Christians are distributed along a continuum from very healthy brains that are securely attached to very unhealthy brains prone to physical and psychiatric disorders. It is the charge of Christians, as members of the body of Christ, to be connected to one another and "care" sufficiently for one another to heal. In a Christian perspective, this healing takes place through common liturgy, prayer, and meditation. Throughout this text, we will try to explain how "grace" builds on "nature."

As a social organism, our brain is composed of billions of neurons that are linked to one another in a marvelous manner to communicate information through synaptic connections. But if we do not use the cells, they are pruned away and die (Jensen 2008). In a similar manner, the brain thrives on stimulating interactions with others. Attachment provides the connections with others and, according to

Cozolino (2006), is the "social synapse," the space between us and others. It provides the link between us and other organisms such as tribes, families, grandparents, siblings, states, and governments.

In attachment connections, we smile, gesture, and say good-morning, etc. Such connections are transmitted through sight, sounds, touches, and words. These messages are received in our sensory system and changed into electrochemical impulses in our highly evolved brains. The resulting signals are processed and stimulate new behaviors, transmitting new messages back across the social synapse.

Our very survival depends on being wired to connect to those around us through our sensory system: sights, odors, touches, and especially words. When there are abnormalities of the sensory systems, attachment communication tends to become impaired.

This brings to mind the story of Helen Keller. Helen showed many of the behavioral problems of being insecurely attached (that we will refer to later). After being struck blind and deaf from an infant illness (likely scarlet fever or meningitis), she eventually became a prolific writer and activist. What is significant about this story is that she recovered from the behavioral problems through a prolonged relationship (forty-nine years) with Anne Sullivan, her governess and companion (Hermann and Macleod, 2007). It seems to have been the attachment connection between the two that enabled Helen to restore a damaged brain and become such an accomplished woman. If there are available nurturing persons who are primed to accept us as extensions of themselves, we can connect, attach, and develop healthy brains, as we will see later. This most marvelous process allows us to survive and continue to connect with others in rewarding ways.

As we grow from infancy to old age, we strengthen our connections with our families, friends, and organizations. In this fruitful process, our brains also grow new neurons and new neural circuits, building functional networks. It is the bonds of attachment and love that make possible healthy and resilient brains.

Insecure attachment and connections result in brains that are at high risk for dysfunctional stress, poor regulation of emotions, and often physical and psychiatric illnesses. Bowlby (1973) documents clinical cases of anxiety and depressive disorders with backgrounds of insecure attachment whereas Schore (2003) reports the development of personality disorders. What is reasonable to conclude is that many health problems are related to whether or not we were given the grace of having parents who cared well for us in early infancy, especially the first year of life.

When attachment is insecure, we often see children with angry, oppositional behavior. They develop a high need for control simply because they cannot trust that parental attachment figures will take care of their needs and dangers. They may be superficially charming but show indiscriminate affection to strangers since they do not know who to trust. They often resist affection from parents and other adults, squirming and avoiding situations where they might expect hugs and the like. They lie about the obvious when no punishment is about to happen since it is a good way to control and confuse adults. They incessantly ask nonsense questions and produce much senseless chatter in order to control and irritate adults. They often show poor eye contact for the age and situation regardless of cultural norms. Perhaps the eyes are the windows of the soul, and they need to protect themselves from anyone looking in to see the anger and pain.

Sometimes we will see very pushy and demanding behavior simply because they can't trust that caretakers will fulfill their needs and threats. They also are seen stealing whatever they can get their hands on, especially sweet things like candy. After all, if they can't trust that adults care for them, they have to take what they believe will help them survive. They seem to lack personal property boundaries simply because the ego has not developed sufficiently to feel good about self in order to share things with others. One of the most severe deficits is the poor ability to regulate feelings and emotions. As a result, they show destructive and aggressive behavior to others and get easily agitated. In none of these conduct problems do they seem to show guilt. They have very poor ability to understand how another would feel if they were hurt or had their property stolen.

The same children show poor verbal development. After all, crying is the beginning of functional language, and it did not "work" when they were infants. Consequently, they often are diagnosed at school age with learning disabilities, especially expressive language and reading disorders (Beischel 2010).

Of special importance for this book is the fact that these children have poor ability to form social relationships and intimacy but are good at superficial relationships. They do not seem able to enjoy other people so that they spend much effort in developing short-term relationships so that they can use others to get their needs met.

Unfortunately, we also frequently see fire setting, enuresis and encopresis, and cruelty to animals. These three behaviors are often associated with the development of sociopathic or psychopathic tendencies. Yet few professionals look at attachment insecurity as precursors of criminal behavior.

My experience of thirty years of work with the insecurely attached and as a psychologist in the Nebraska State Penitentiary suggests that it is critical early development that motivates the beginnings of antisocial behavior. If we add subsequent poor parenting and traumatic violence to insecurity of attachment, we have a pretty good formula for developing antisocial people (Lewis, Mallouh, and Webb 1989). This does not rule out that there are differing genetic predispositions for security of attachment, but it does suggest that security of attachment is a high-risk factor for the development of antisocial behavior. Just looking at genetics and, later (after eighteen months of age), parenting is not sufficient. This is why we believe that attachment theory is a better way to look at healthy and unhealthy development.

So in this book, we will trace what happens to our brains when we are not properly cared for and how social relations in a Christian context can begin the healing process—the recovery of the brain. We will especially emphasize the historical importance of a relationship with God in calming down the agitated mind of the insecurely attached. It is the mandate of our contract with God that we reach out to the insecurely attached to care for them rather than devaluing and rejecting them.

We will present the case of how mindfulness training and stimulation of the relaxation response through prayer and meditation have great potential for calming down the damaged brains of those who have early histories of insecurity of attachment and trauma.

Introduction

The Story of David Begins

I MET DAVID FOR THE first time when he was brought to my office by Margaret Moore, his caseworker at the Nebraska Department of Social Services. This was over thirty-nine years ago, long before much of the evidence contained in this book was available, including the neuroimaging brain studies. David almost immediately stuck out his hand while smiling in an exaggerated fashion and said, "Hello, Dr. Beischel, I'm David North." I was immediately thinking what a well-behaved boy he was when he darted toward my computer. Not knowing what might happen to my computer if he got to it, I blocked his approach and said, "David, that is my computer, and you can only use it if I say so, and right now, I would like you to sit down next to Ms. Moore so that I can get to know you." We thus began the tug-of-war about who was going to have control of this session. I am sure now that David wanted and expected to be able to control me and the session. I did my best to set boundaries in my office space.

Between David and Ms. Moore, I was filled in with a terrible history of neglect and abuse. At one point, David pulled up his pant leg to show me the cigarette-burn scars and pulled down the back collar of his shirt to show me that the scars went from his heels to the nape of his neck.

David lived in his home at a survival level, stealing food and cruising around his neighborhood with no understanding of personal boundaries. He also showed almost no ability to regulate his anger. If he did not get what he wanted, he would throw temper tantrums and kick holes through the drywall in his home. When he was younger, he was kept tied in his crib in an attempt to keep him under control. If all else failed, he was tortured with the cigarette burns. The session ended with my dismay at his supersilly grin and extreme need for control. We had just begun years of work together.

1

Development of the Brain

FROM THE OUTSET, IT IS important to understand that our behavior is created or altered through an intricate connection of nerves from perceptual stimulation and brain processing, eventually ordering a specific motor response. Some brains process information quite adaptively and others in ways that are not socially acceptable. During the first year of life, the foundation of a healthy or unhealthy brain is being set.

When the environment for an infant is "uncaring" and violent, the brain does not develop in a healthy manner. For several decades now, neurobiology has been looking at the early beginnings of adult psychopathology. When an infant enters an unhealthy environment, the brain develops differently in both neurochemistry and brain organization. What seems most affected is the brain's regulatory system, including affect regulation.

When an infant expresses emotions such as crying, "uncaring" adults may either overrespond or underrespond. An appropriate parent does something to moderate the emotional state such as feeding, rocking, hugging, talking to the infant so that the negative emotional state is modulated into positive affect. If the parent is less "available" or feels less attached, she/he may overrespond in anger and traumatize the infant or underrespond by neglecting to do anything. The above-described "over" or "under" response has been termed by Schore (2003) as *relational trauma*. Most scientists now recognize that psychiatric disorders are caused by a combination of genetic predisposition and environmental stressors. Genetic predispositions are turned "on" or "off" or altered through the environment. Relational trauma is both qualitatively and quantitatively one of the strongest factors in determining later behavior.

The infant brain is very vulnerable to the environment because, by its nature, it is social. We like to think that most people take good care of their infants. The work of Mary Ainsworth (Ainsworth et al. 1978) suggests that this is true about 60 percent of the time. This means that about 40 percent of the time, parents are at risk of engineering unsafe environments for infants, leading to insecure patterns of attachment. The research on infant deaths, neglect, and abuse clearly suggest that the work of Ainsworth is credible.

To understand what goes wrong in the brains of the insecure, we need to understand a bit about how the brain works. As we gain more knowledge from neuroscience, it is apparent that the human brain has evolved into a very complex organ of information processing. We will now try to simplify that knowledge for our purposes in this book.

In order to understand how we think and feel, the two most important areas of the brain are the limbic system and the frontal lobe. When we have histories of early "relational trauma," both of these systems are poorly developed. Physically, the limbic system lies just below the cerebral cortex and just behind the frontal lobe. For the most part, it includes the hypothalamus, the hippocampus, and the amygdala.

The Limbic System

The *hypothalamus* is sort of a thermostat. It keeps the brain and body at a "set point." It regulates hunger, thirst, pain, pleasure, anger, aggression, and more. It also regulates physical body processes such as pulse, blood pressure, and breathing. Of special interest in this book, the hypothalamus also regulates arousal in response to emotional situations. If the hypothalamus does not work optimally, regulation of emotional responses is affected. It is harder to get emotions back to the set point. The insecurely attached get angrier or sadder or overexcited and stay in extreme emotional states longer. This is part of the reason that Foster Cline (1979) called the insecurely attached *the children of rage.*

The *hippocampus* got its name due to the fact that it is sort of shaped like a sea horse. One of its primary functions is to organize and index information for storage in long-term memory. When the organism is under stress, the hormone cortisol is secreted. This is an energy source to help us defeat the source of the stress: to escape or attack. But when we can't get rid of the stress for week or months, cortisol becomes toxic, especially to the hippocampus. With prolonged exposure to cortisol, neurons (brain cells) in the hippocampus die (Jensen 2008). We see this in chronic post-traumatic stress victims from war or abuse. They have trouble keeping memories from the past. Anxious and stressed individuals are often quite "forgetful." This is one of the problems of the reports of abuse victims. Because they can't remember well, they creatively fill in the gaps with bits and pieces from other memories. We often see these memory deficits in depressed and anxious patients also.

The *amygdala* is also part of the limbic system, located at the lower end of the hippocampus. It is a key player in emotional arousal. It seems to code and identify emotional arousal. When it is electrically stimulated in animals, they become very aggressive; but when it is removed, there is almost no reaction to situations that in the past would have resulted in aggression. Similarly, it also seems to be involved in fear and sexual responses. The amygdala also plays an important role in defining a stimulus and, thereby, responding adaptively. Also, our social behavior is partially determined by the amygdala, so evaluation of faces and distinguishing trust from betrayal is partially accomplished through a healthy amygdala. When the amygdala is hyperactive, we see abnormalities of being able to trust those who are trustworthy. This may partially explain why insecurely attached individuals end up trusting those who harm them and not trusting those who attempt to nurture and care for them. Our emotional behavior is greatly determined by the amygdala.

In summary, the limbic system is the arousal system of the brain. It stimulates and regulates emotional responses. What we have found out in recent years is that when individuals suffer from relational trauma, the limbic system becomes hyperactive (Jensen 2008) and overresponds to sensory stimuli. An accidental bumping of someone results in a physical attack in these children. In adults, we see the slightest insult or perceived lack of importance as reason for paranoid or excessive verbal attack on others. And some of the time, these individuals can become violent and seriously dangerous.

I remember well a teenage patient of mine. Stephanie was a rather large twelve-year-old in the sixth grade at a local Omaha junior high school. I had been seeing her for sometime in therapy, working on security and safety issues. She needed to learn to trust parents and teachers but had a long way to go. We had not gotten very far in therapy when a tragic even occurred. On a particular day, Stephanie was in an art class. The teacher, Ms. Spencer, was having the students cut out designs with scissors to glue onto background paper. Stephanie was quite ambivalent in her feeling toward people who had authority over her: one minute needing excessive attention and the next in rage and anger.

Ms. Spencer was helping Stephanie with her design, and so Stephanie felt a sense of connection and protection. But when the teacher had to go to another student to help them, Stephanie felt abandoned and enraged. By now, the teacher was bent over with her back exposed. Stephanie jumped up and stabbed her teacher, planting the scissors two to three inches in her exposed back. Although the teacher survived, Stephanie was on her way to a local psychiatric hospital and juvenile court. This uncontrolled rage is frequently seen in violence toward adoptive and foster parents.

The Frontal Lobe

Although the cortex of the brain involves a number of areas or lobes, for our purposes we will focus on the frontal lobe. The frontal lobe is located right behind the forehead and eyes. Although there are many connections to other parts of the brain, we have generally thought of the frontal lobe as the center of "thinking." Part of the frontal lobe is involved in motor association. When there is damage in this area, we do not lose all motor behavior but rather the coordination of smooth integration of complex movements. Movements become spasmodic and poorly coordinated. We see this in the walking gait of brain-damaged individuals (Filskov et al. 1981).

We are specifically interested in the prefrontal area due to its involvement in emotional regulation and social functioning. Luria (1969) saw the prefrontal cortex as an "executive" control center. This original term led to a great deal of research and the developing of psychological-testing instruments on the "executive functions" of the brain. Although this body of research does not exactly list the same functions, we will turn to Russell Barkley (2012) for a current listing and understanding of these abilities or functions. He has concluded that instead of clear functions, we can identify eight emerging developmental capacities.

The general capacity is the ability to select goals and problem-solving the means to achieve the goals. The first capacity is *spatial*: the distance over which one is planning to accomplish a self-directed goal. This is originally physical and eventually becomes social. As children grow and develop, they see and extend the environment that they must organize and arrange to accomplish the goal. When this ability is impaired, as in those suffering from relational trauma, these individuals do not see all the physical and social variables that they must rearrange in order to accomplish the goal. When children and adults do not suffer from relational trauma, they readily accept corrections and new perceptions from parents, spouses, friends, and others with whom they have secure relationships.

The second capacity is *temporal*: how far into the future a person can keep their mind on a goal. Sometimes the window between choosing a goal and accomplishing it is quite short and sometimes very long. Developmentally, as the prefrontal cortex matures, we can keep our mind on goals for longer and longer periods of time. This tracking ability is impaired with the insecurely attached. They simply can't keep "in mind" what they want or poorly assess the time interval, so they often look for short-term goals or want things to happen more quickly than possible. This leaves those suffering from relational trauma with poor ability to be patient. When they don't get what they want immediately, they get frustrated and angry. Waiting their turn in lines often leads to aggressive, inappropriate social behavior. This explains to some extent why we see these people in young adulthood choosing activities such as drug dealing and prostitution, which have very quick reward times.

Another executive capacity is motivational: the emotional arousal concerning the goals they are planning. The more one values a proposed goal, the more one will be willing to delay gratification and be patient in terms of space and time. If one is impaired in developing a value for a goal, they will not be willing to work for the goal over time and space. We see those with relational trauma finding it difficult to balance the "wanting" of the goal with the time and distance from the goal. This again impels them to choose short-term goals or poorly asses the accomplishment of longer (in space and time) goals.

If you don't really want to get an A in a course, you certainly won't do the necessary work to accomplish getting the A. As a result, they are often observed as "unmotivated" to caring parents and teachers. The brain is out of balance, and no rewards system seems to be very effective in motivating the insecurely attached and traumatized students or workers.

I used to see a boy like this who sat in a six-foot square bounded by white tape in a form of "time-out." He refused to do any chores or homework and instead sat in the square with his arms folded, an angry frown on his face, day after day. One of the first goals of therapy was to pull up the tape and begin again working on an adaptive relationship between the boy and his adoptive mother.

The next executive capacity listed by Barkley (2012) is *inhibitory*: being able to subordinate their immediate interests for the sake of attaining the goal. Those who have poor ability to do so are viewed as "impulsive," "selfish," or perhaps "stupid." They have to be able to inhibit a current drive in order to accomplish the longer goal. Those who have been through relational trauma are not able to do this well.

When presented with a box of very attractive toys and told that she could pick one, such a girl responded, "I choose them all," and grabbed the box in an attempt to escape. She could not choose one without realizing that they were all attractive and could not inhibit the desire to have more than one gift.

Because of this deficit, birthdays were very difficult for our adopted children. When the birthday boy or girl received birthday gifts, the others would become very angry. They appeared quite selfish and egocentric when they could not be happy for their brother or sister. No explanation of how they also would get gifts when it was their birthday helped. They simply could not wait for their turn. The lack of this capacity results in many behavior problems at home and at school.

Conceptual/abstract capacity is used in goal attainment when we apply rules to getting what we want. To get a goal, sometimes we apply simple social rules such as, "Wait for your turn." But sometimes the rules are more abstract such as, "Respect the rights of others," or "Don't overstep the physical boundaries of others." We are continually using rules like these in our social behavior. Those who have been exposed to relational trauma have poor ability to flexibly apply such principles when planning to accomplish goals. Listening to antisocial children and adults, as I have done for thirty years, has made it abundantly clear that this capacity is missing or poorly developed. This, of course, lessens the ability to "freely" control raging emotions and impulsive behavior. Most people, especially court workers, do not understand that the insecurely attached can go into a rage, which may last for many hours, when rejected. I once did an evaluation on an insecurely attached young man who killed five people in a span of about ten hours. In a rage, he attempted to kill the young lady who "broke up" with him. Although he legally ended up with a death sentence, it is another question of how God would judge him.

Social capacity is equally impaired after relational trauma. This includes the group of people that the individual interacts with at work, home, and in recreation. It includes being able to reciprocate and cooperate in accomplishing tasks with these individuals. Many of the relationally traumatized have very superficial relationships with friends, relatives, and coworkers. It is always interesting to look at their multiple partners and job settings. The circuits in the right orbital frontal area of the brain, as seen through neuroimaging, wither and die without mutual interactions (Cozolina 2010).

When there is no one there to respond to the crying infant, the crying eventually stops. The social circuits that allow us to be rewarded in social situations appear to be missing in those who have been neglected early in life. I remember seeing an eighteen-month-old who came from an extremely neglecting environment. The response system never developed, so she stopped crying when she had needs or was threatened. The adoptive parents reported that she no longer cried or made any protest when they accidentally stuck her leg with safety pins in diapering her. She is now an adult who has had many, many partners and simply cannot do the give-and-take required for intimacy. The social capacity to interact with positive feelings and the ability to cooperate with others and set limits and boundaries do not develop properly in the relationally traumatized.

Cultural capacity is the ability to extract and use cultural information to solve problems and make decisions. One has to have a brain that is able to receive the information and apply it in a current setting. When this executive function is weak or nonexistent, the reciprocal ability to receive and transmit the culture does not work well. Cultural information is thought to be the means to accomplish goals more readily, but when the reciprocity is missing, this is not easily accomplished. Cultural identity has to be in place in order to take advantage of one's culture in goal accomplishment. With the insecurely attached, identity is often diffuse, and cultural norms are used for survival but easily abandoned without a healthy ego housed in the frontal cortex. Cultural norms and identity have to be learned but often happens very poorly due to distrust of parental figures.

In some homes, cultural norms, including religion, are hypocritically expressed. What their parents and church say is inconsistent with behavior. The epitome of this in the Catholic Church is the priest pedophile, who preaches caring for others on one hand and hurts children when opportunity arises on the other. Cultural capacity is based on a healthy ego with a healthy and consistent experience of the culture. We see the eight EF to be more available in healthy humans. They have resilient brains readily capable of accomplishing goals over time and space. On the other hand, we see the relationally traumatized unable to effectively accomplish goals, sometimes even the simplest of goals. One of the reasons is that the brain is social, but their social capacity is diminished as we have already suggested. Later we will say that it is the imperative of the healthy to lift up the unhealthy in religious cooperation through liturgical celebrations, prayer, and social action.

Neurotransmitters messages move through our brain from neuron to neuron, forming circuits and networks of neurons. Between the neurons, there are chemicals called neurotransmitters that either promote or inhibit the communication. For the brain to work properly, there has to be balance of these neurotransmitters. During the first year of life, these neurotransmitters get balanced through the attachment process (Hart 2011). This involves the noradrenaline-serotonin-dopamine systems. These neurotransmitters have to be available to support healthy brain functioning. Studies of young monkeys who grew up in isolation or with surrogate mothers have shown low levels of noradrenalin with a despair response to separation (Kraemer 1992). This explains well how the insecurely attached show an extreme sense of loss and depression, especially on the adolescent and adult level. Low levels of noradrenalin are also associated with the ability to maintain attention, motivation, and persistence (Hart 2011). This, of course, would explain poor school functioning and perhaps, part of the reason for learning disabilities in the insecurely attached.

Dopamine levels are also lower in these individuals. Dopamine is responsible for a sense of reward and happiness and has been termed the "feel-good" neurotransmitter. The hollow, sad eyes of institutionalized children in orphanages are likely related to this deficit.

Lower serotonin levels are also found in insecurely attached children and adults. The serotonin levels are also regulated through security of attachment. When attachment is insecure with lower levels of serotonin, we tend to see more aggressive and depressive behavior (Hart 2011). This then affects the regulation of sadness, anger, and excitement.

DNA is also compromised by living highly stressed lives. Telomeres are a protective casing at the end of a DNA strand. Cortisol exposure from chronic stress tends to diminish the telomeres. This results eventually in cell death, or the cell becomes pro-inflammatory. This is the explanation of why we often see health-related stress disorders: heart disease, stroke, cancer, etc. Recent studies have indicated that individuals with shorter telomeres are also more likely to experience shrinkage of the hippocampus and consequently memory and immune problems (*Mind, Mood & Memory* 2015).

Some recent studies (Lu 2014) indicate that anxious mothers bring into the world infants with shorter telomeres. This might explain the multiple health-related disorders seen in insecurely attached children and adults. "Maltreatment, abuse, severe neglect and exposure to violence all seem to take a swath from the telomeres" (LU 2014). So one of the biological factors in the insecurely attached is likely damaged DNA.

In summary, the development of the brain and nervous system is greatly affected by relational trauma. As mentioned earlier, security of attachment is a prerequisite for the development of a healthy brain. One of the premises of this book is that it is not just that some people have healthy brains and other have unhealthy brains, but rather that individuals are distributed across the continuum of attachment security and that, together, we join one another to heal our deficits. This we will discuss next in presenting our understanding of the social brain and intimacy development.

David's Brain

We now return to our story of David. If the above research is correct, we would expect to see David having an overresponsive limbic system and a poorly developed frontal lobe with resulting weaknesses in the executive functions. David's many parents all complained of David's poor impulse control and memory processes. He had to be continually reminded of chores, homework, etc. At the time, this was interpreted as due to being "oppositional"; but some of the time, it was likely due to poor recall. This was likely due to living in a highly aroused limbic state with cortisol destroying cells in the hippocampus. In kindergarten, he had to be tutored at night to learn the ABCs, although psychological testing showed an above average IQ.

He never learned in early childhood to cooperate and share with parents or other children. He always saw others as "dangerous" and out to hurt him, and so he often attacked first. Soon his little peers figured out that it would be "fun" to get him going and out of control. So a group of them would bait him into angry displays. One day I was driving past his school just as school left out and saw him in a confrontation with about six other boys. They were calling him names, and he was flailing back with his schoolbag full of books. His parents at the time were always wondering why they had to buy him new schoolbags frequently. We now had the answer.

Because of his high need for control and poor ability to control his emotions, when he was forced to do things such as homework and chores, he became very angry. Early in life, this was manifested in temper tantrums; at school age, as destructive behavior. One time his desk was cleaned out by his parents, and they found a dozen pencils broken in half, about fifty broken crayons, torn papers, and about eight scissors (possible weapons). Much of these items were, of course, stolen from other children. He never understood how other children would feel and react to his stealing. The orbital frontal areas of the brain, where social judgment and problem solving take place, had not developed sufficiently to inhibit the stealing.

Finally, David was often ill, likely due to the damaged hippocampus and its role in the immune system. Perhaps this was also related to the shortened telomeres as indicated above. He was diagnosed with mild heart irregularities as a child.

When David arrived in his adoptive home, he showed a lot of anxious behavior. He licked his lips almost constantly and stretched the tissue around his mouth. The continuous exaggerated smiling, stretching, and licking produced dry, cracked lips. Eventually this resulted in cracking of the lips that had to be surgically repaired several times. In the first months, he also suffered from enuresis (urinating in bed at night). As he adjusted to the new adoptive home, the enuresis stopped, but he was still orally fixated, gorging on food and stealing food. The first meal in the adopted home was hamburgers. Before anyone else could sit down for dinner, David pulled out a hamburger from the bun and shoved it whole into his mouth. While the rest of the family were getting seated, David was already swallowing the burger with only a few chews. Mel, his foster father (later adoptive father), could not believe his eyes and said, "Slow down, David, or you will get sick eating in such a hurry." David's limbic system was in full gear, and so he hardly heard his father. He was ready for a second burger. It wasn't long before David very appropriately excused himself to go to the bathroom. Mel and Lea, his foster mom, did not have the slightest idea that he was vomiting, not having a bowel movement. It took about a month before they realized that David had an eating disorder.

One of the first issues of therapy was David's eating. The problem was resolved in time through the mirror neurons and social learning theory. David could not pick up his fork until Mel did so. Mel cut his meat into small pieces, and David followed suit. It always amazed me that an oppositional child like David would follow every move of Mel. Perhaps it had to do with past abuse and the need to follow the model of a kind and low-key parent. Whatever it was, it worked. Although he still ate at a very fast rate, the extreme gorging stopped. Both Mel, Lea, and myself (the therapist) sighed approval and relief.

2

The Social Brain and the Development of Intimacy

WHEN WE LOOK AT THE evolution of species, we soon become aware that not all animal species survive. Often the reason for not surviving is due to social behavior. A pride of lions can kill an antelope by cornering it, but a single lion is too slow to kill a healthy antelope. The human brain has evolved as a very sophisticated social organ. Healthy brains need family, relatives, and friends to survive. When attachment is insecure, these connections are impaired, and the brain itself does not develop into a healthy and adaptive organ of survival. In short, we need many eyes, ears, and hands helping us overcome the stresses of living. We need grocery stores, contractors, police departments, city and federal governments, employers in order to provide for food, housing, and protection from our predators. In primates, the cortex has gotten larger in the evolution of species in order to handle larger and larger social groups due to the need for complex communication, problem solving, and abstracting abilities (Cozolino 2010).

As the cortex evolved in man, there was also the corresponding development of specialized tasks, such as hunting, gathering, fighting, and prolonged caretaking. In most larger mammals, programming of the brain is genetic so that the offspring are ready to survive with little help from the parent and less need for early caretaking. In humans, the brain is a work in development, very much dependent on parental care. When this parental care is of poor quality (relational trauma), the brain itself does not develop in a healthy manner, as discussed in chapter 1. Because man is a much more sophisticated animal than a lion, it takes many more years to learn the complexities of the social groups. This, in turn, precipitated the development of a very complex language system. The evolution of complex relationships, language, and cortical space allowed for higher levels of symbolic and abstract thinking (Cozolino 2010), already discussed under the executive functions in chapter 1.

In the last century, it was noted that many children in orphanages were dying. At the time, physicians assumed that they were dying due to the spread of microorganisms.

As a result, they separated the children and minimized the staff handling of the children. Their hypothesis failed, and the children continued to die. Later they came up with a social hypothesis: holding, playing with consistent caretakers, and allowing the children to interact with one another. This hypothesis worked, and the death rate went down (Blum 2002). Social connections are needed for survival.

Bowlby (1969, 1982) hypothesized that when parents were not consistently available to respond to the cries of infants, an insecure form of attachment resulted, characterized by expectations of self and others. What the caretaker would do in different situations was impaired. At some point, the infant's cries turn into despair. Because no one comes, the infant no longer expects the parent to come and care for the child. During this first year of life, the beginning of an ego, or self, is formed. If no one comes, it must be because "I am not worthy of being cared for or loved." The real insecurity of damaged attachment is the fear of not surviving. As a result, the ego is always questioning that others cannot be counted on to help them fulfill their needs or overcome an environmental danger. These fears and anxieties interfere with the development of intimacy. Later in this book, we will explain how the resolution of these fears and anxieties is through a relationship with God. Intimacy with God is promoted through learning how to communicate with Him through prayer, meditation, and social action.

Intimacy begins with the very first interactions between mother and child. There appears to be a biological capacity for an infant to imitate the mother's behavior: the mirror neurons located in the premotor areas of the frontal cortex. These neurons were first discovered in research with monkeys (Cozolino 2010). The researchers found out that specific neurons fired when a related behavior was observed, but the neurons also fired when the animal imitated the behavior. These neurons are present in human infants at birth. As almost any mother can tell you, infants readily imitate behavior such as mouth movements. Eventually they will be very important in rapid acquisition of language. More recently (Hart 2011), it has been discovered that these mirror neurons are also located in the parietal lobes. This enables the infant not only to imitate the attachment figure's behavior but also to understand the other person's intent in performing the motor actions. At some point, we become part of the other and often try to help the other. This phenomenon is operative when we lean to help a tightwire walker stay balanced. This mutuality of intent is already happening between mother and infant as they attune to each other.

The attunement takes place between mother and infant through the mutual regulation of arousal. In order to accomplish this, the mother has to be sensitive to changes in the infant's states. The infant then responds to the mother's attempt to activate and reduce arousal. These interactions produce neural circuits that are the basis of the capacity for self-regulation. When a parent is not sensitive and responsive in attempting to regulate affect, the capacity for self-regulation is minimized. Parents who are themselves insecurely attached tend to be so self-absorbed that they are neither sensitive nor responsive to their infant's needs. Their infants, in turn, do not develop the brain organization required for affect regulation and remain in negative affect states with little neural capacity to regulate. They grow up to be insensitive adults who have emotional regulation problems. This cycle goes on and on generation after generation.

When the insecurely attached become adults, a major deficit is in the ability to have emotional intimacy in relationships. Although the concept of "intimacy" has slightly different meaning for different authors, we believe there are certain skills involved: self-awareness, empathy, communication of emotions, conflict resolution, and the ability to sustain commitments (Papalia et al. 2004).

Self-awareness requires a healthy ego. The insecure ego is continually doubting that it is "lovable" and worthy of care. This often results in the need to make up stories so that one looks better than one believes they are. The perception of self is so low that this continuous need for attention results in frequent change of partners, jobs, and activities. The fluctuating ego states are very confusing to others and often result in the termination of relationships.

In order to have empathy, a person must be able to take the other's position—to be able to look at an emotion or situation from another's perspective. Empathic thinking requires emotional attunement, and the affect regulation (Cozolino 2010), which we have indicated, is impaired in the insecurely attached. They tend to be so overconcerned about getting their own needs met that they cannot pull back from their own current needs in order to imagine how another might feel in this situation. When the insecurely attached commit crimes, they are concerned about their needs (freedom from punishment) and never get concerned about how the victim felt. Courts and judges often are looking for such empathy but will only find faked attempts to express empathy. In a relationship, both partners have to be able to regulate their own perception of needs and pay attention to their partner's needs from time to time. When the attunement is missing, we find that the give-and-take around needs is often impaired.

In order to communicate emotions, individuals have to know themselves and how they are feeling here and now. As indicated above, the insecurely attached have very low self-esteem and highly defended egos. Their egos are diffuse and ever changing. When an ego-dystonic remark is made, the insecure person fires back with verbal or physical aggression. This is because they are poor at regulation. Generally they suppress emotions rather than be aware of them due to the poor ability to regulate. Much of communication is about what they would like to feel rather than what they actually feel. When they say "I love you," what they often really mean is "I need you" or "I want to control you." In terms of

Maslow (1968), their needs' development is at the survival or physiological level.

To resolve a conflict, both parties must be able to regulate affect and be sensitive to the other party's position. The insecurely attached just want their needs met at all costs due to the fear of not surviving. They want to take and not give. To be sensitive to another's position means that you have to be empathic and sensitive. When the brain has developed in a manner that does not support affect regulation and empathic sensitivity, conflict resolution and negotiation quickly degenerates into arguing and fighting.

Finally, to accomplish intimacy, there has to be an ability to sustain commitments. We live in a fast-paced world that is in continuous flux. We purchase, partially use, and throw away. One of the major problems environmentally is waste products and their disposal. If we do not know who we are and where we are going, we start many things and then throw them away. If the ego is not well developed, we readily start relationships and easily end them. If we regulate emotions poorly, cannot work out conflicts well, and are poorly attuned to partners and attachment objects, we are likely to easily quit relationships.

When I evaluate adults for attachment insecurity, I often ask them to list the significant relationships and jobs begun and ended in the past ten years. It is not unusual to see multiple marriages and many friendships and jobs made and broken. In summary, among the insecure, intimacy ability is a major deficit in having happy, productive lives.

3

Anxiety and Fear

EVOLUTIONARY THEORY SUGGESTS THAT WE are biologically organized to survive and pass our genes on to the next generation. Our brains and sensory system are wired to recognize danger. Anxiety and fear are the conscious interpretation of our ongoing appraisal of threat and danger. Some fears may be biologically organized, such as fear of snakes and spiders, heights, etc. The fight-or-flight circuitry of the autonomic nervous system may be more biological, but it is connected to the frontal area where we can learn new fears and anxieties, and so often do.

When we experience this complex array of fears and anxieties, our bodies and brains are being prepared to avoid the perceived danger. To avoid the rattlesnake on the trail, we either have to run or attack the snake very quickly. In order to do so, our bodies make some quick changes. Energy has to be available in our cardiovascular and muscle system, as well as in brain regions.

Increases in blood supply to our large muscles, as well as epinephrine and the glucocorticoids, prepare us for quick action that we cannot accomplish when in a more relaxed state. With the emergence of imagination, we are also able to fear and worry about imagined dangers that may never happen. What was designed as an alarm system can become a nuisance (Cozolino 2010).

We have two fear circuits available: fast and slow. The fast system sends information through the thalamus (the gatekeeper of the brain) to the amygdala, where the data is translated into behaviors via the autonomic nervous system. The slow system simultaneously routes the data to the hippocampus and cortex for more assessment. This process is slower due to the many synaptic connections in the cortex and the multiple circuits of past memories in the hippocampus. It is here that the decision-making of the executive functions (see chapter 1) are activated. This dual system explains why we instinctively respond to a perceived danger before we consciously recognize that it is not a danger. If it is, in fact, a real danger—such as a bomb exploding at the Boston Marathon race—the fast processing serves us well as we escape the area.

Although we may be genetically organized to fear things like snakes, explosions, loud noises, etc., we can pair any thought, sensation, or feeling with a noxious stimuli, such as loud noises and bright lights. As a result, we can learn to be anxious in many situations in life. Infants need to have caring adults to help them regulate negative affect. Yelling, screaming, and loud noises in families prone to violence sets the stage for such pairing and the development of anxieties. When this early care is lacking, as in infants who are going through neglect and abuse, the whole neural infrastructure is changed. As mentioned earlier, the limbic system tends to become hyperactive and overresponsive even before the development of the frontal structures. Unconscious fears and anxieties have their roots in disorganized and violent homes.

As mentioned earlier, prolonged stress from family violence and neglect affects two processes: protein production and hippocampal damage (Cozolino 2010). Proteins are the building blocks of our immune system. When we work with anxious and depressed individuals, it is common to see many other health problems. Since the hippocampus regulates and organizes short-term memory for storage, the hippocampal damage results also in poor ability to inhibit emotions. The hippocampus is also very sensitive to oxygen deprivation and may be damaged by any other brain damage resulting in anoxia, such as prolonged and difficult births. Due to deficits in ego development, relationally traumatized adults do not take good care of themselves during pregnancy and bring forth infants at risk for hippocampal deficits.

One of the anomalies of nature is that the limbic system, especially the amygdala, is mature before birth, but the frontal lobe takes until young adulthood (Pribram 1997). It is primarily the frontal area of the cortex that is capable of inhibiting the impulses of the limbic system. So we are born crying with poor ability to regulate the negative affect states (Schore 2003). So infants come into a hostile world. They are at risk from overwhelming fear with poor ability to calm themselves down. But we have also evolved with a system to regulate the fear: attachment. Infants are biologically organized to use proximity to parents to regulate the fear. Not only do they learn to regulate fear and anxiety by trusting adults to protect and care for them, they also develop a more efficient brain that can regulate their own fears as they develop into adulthood.

It is through this first relationship that the foundation for regulating fear and anxiety is established. When the attachment system is not readily available, we see the opposite: children and adults with brains that are out of balance. The relationally traumatized have hyperactive limbic systems that respond to sensory stimulation with survival fear, unable to calm themselves down, and at great risk for depression, anxiety, and physical disorders as Bowlby (1973) has suggested. It is the hyperactive brain that has to be calmed down through relationships. In the following chapters, we will attempt to explain how a relationship with God through the mystical body of Christ is one way of accomplishing this.

David in Adolescence

David grew physically in early adolescence and was a large boy now, over six feet tall and weighing over two hundred pounds. Mel, his adopted father, had played college basketball and so began working with David around a hoop he had erected in the back driveway. David loved the one-on-one attention he got in practicing with Mel. When working with Mel, David looked almost supernormal. When Mel was not there, David went into survival mode. David got lots of attention as the starting center on the freshman basketball team. He was an indomitable force under the basket.

When David was not playing basketball and under the control of a coach or Mel, he resorted to survival mode. Peers continued to make fun of David, and he roared back in anger. He was intermittently praised and punished due to poor social skills. He continued to have boundary problems, stealing from his peers whom he wanted to like him. When he snuck into the locker room and took money from the wallets of his own teammates, he was thrown off the team. Although he wished that he could, Mel was not able to avert the consequences of David's stealing. This began the long history of juvenile court appearances. Mel and Lea were confused and spent many hours dealing with their own feelings over this turn of events.

When Lea asked David to do anything, he got angry and stomped off. He would run away and then call Mel to come and pick him up. When they returned home, Lea was angry at both. Eventually Mel and Lea worked through these issues.

4

Attachment and Mental Health

IN SOCIAL SCIENCE LITERATURE, THERE has been a rebirth of interest in religion and spirituality up against the secularization of religion emanating from the work of Marx, Durkheim, and Weber (Ellison and McFarland 2013). This has opened the door for more thorough study of religion and spirituality from a social science perspective. Far from the prediction of Nietzsche (1883–1885) that God is dead is a resurgent interest in religion. It is now estimated that, worldwide, 85 percent of people report having religious beliefs (Zukerman 2005).

There has been a broad array of behaviors studied that have verified that a belief and perceived interaction with supernatural agents such as "gods" improves a wide variety of health issues. The research includes longer life, fewer depressive symptoms, higher levels of prosocial behavior, better marital functioning, less crime and drug use, and higher school achievement (McCullough and Carter 2013). We believe that it is due to the development of self-control over emotions and drives. As man evolved from a nomadic lifestyle to a more stable, sedentary agrarian style, self-control became more important. Waiting, tolerating, and cooperating require that we have certain executive functions available "under the label of self-control" (McCullough and Carter 2013).

The above anthropological argument is bolstered by psychological studies on religion and self-control. Numerous studies on personality and religiosity have confirmed a positive correlation. Measures of religiosity and self-control and self-regulation have also been found to be positively associated. Parents who are religious have children who are rated by both teachers and parents to have higher self-control and lower impulsivity (McCullough and Carter 2013).

When individuals have specific religious beliefs, they tend to set goals and values that are different than nonreligious people. A number of studies taken together suggest that religious people are more likely to have goals related to respecting and concern for others and dissuading goals that support gratification and individuality. It is likely that religious principles end up promoting different goals. Marital partners who had religious beliefs that marriage was a "sacrament" or "sacred" had healthier marriages with better adjustment and conflict resolution. Many of the goals that religious people espouse due to their belief systems require patience, waiting, and cooperation and so require self-control. In this sense, moral deficits or "sin" can be reduced to weakness in self-control and emotional regulation. This does not mean that the relationally traumatized and insecurely attached cannot keep the Ten Commandments or other moral imperatives, but it does suggest that it will be more difficult. And this is why the greatest "grace" is having good parents who care for and nurture us well.

More specific studies on attachment and religion have been done in recent years. The rationale for many of these studies is that we first attach to a primary caregiver and then use that behavioral organization with other attachment objects such as friends, relatives, and teachers. God or other divine figures can function as an attachment figure, at least symbolically. We believe that it is this "connection" that enables people with religion or spirituality to function differently. Granqvist and Kirkpatrick (2008) have reviewed many years of research on attachment, spirituality, and religion. They concluded that the perceived relationship between God and a believer fulfills the requirement for attachment as understood by Bowlby and Ainsworth. They point out that "love" is a dominant emotional theme as in other attachment relationships. People do turn to God as a safe haven when distressed. Because God is eternal and all-powerful, it is the one attachment that we cannot lose. If one believes in an afterlife, they will be with God for all eternity. Separation from God is perceived as *hell* in most Christian belief systems. To be abandoned by God is the "dark night of the soul," as described by St. John of the Cross (Kavanaugh and Rodriquez 1991).

In summary, we have sufficient research and conclusions that attachment to God functions very much like attachment to one's mother or father. The same connection—sense of safety and security and use in times of stress to help in satisfying needs—appears to be present.

5

The Relaxation Response

Dr. Herbert Benson (2010) has been doing research at Harvard University and Massachusetts General Hospital for many years on how "beliefs" are an important factor in health science. Modern medicine has become very dependent on "cure" through surgery and medication, but there is another possibility. There has been considerable research in recent years suggesting that the mind-body approach can be used alone or in combination of traditional medical treatment. Benson's contribution to the mind-body approach is what he has called the *relaxation revolution*.

Benson found out that mental states could significantly change physiologic function. The mind can change body responses. He soon realized that a lot of medical problems were due to stimulation of the autonomic nervous system's fight-or-flight response. He realized that he needed to come up with a reversal of that response. He called it the *relaxation response*.

He sees this response as characterized by decreases in metabolism, heart rate, blood pressure, and breathing rate; calming in brain activity; increase in attention; and changes in gene activity (Benson and Proctor 2010).

Researchers at Harvard found out that they could stimulate this relaxation response through transcendental meditation. The original research showed that the practice of meditation decreased oxygen consumption and respiration rate and increased alpha waves in the brain. Later research using functional magnetic imaging (fMRI) found that subjects who regularly practiced meditation had thicker cortices in the frontal area (Benson and Proctor 2010). This is of special interest to us because of the work of Schore (2003) indicating damage to the right frontal cortex due to relational trauma. This is significant because of the frontal lobe's ability to regulate impulses from the limbic system. This is, perhaps, why people who practice prayer and meditation can calm themselves down and live healthier, more regulated lives.

Benson's (2010) first research was done with hypertension (blood pressure). He first studied how stressors could increase the blood pressure in squirrel monkeys. In the 1960s, this was a revolutionary idea since, prior to this, it was believed that high blood pressure was due to kidney problems. Later studies showed that this was also true of human subjects. He and his colleagues recognized that stressful environments that tend to increase the level of stress hormones and noradrenaline also increased blood pressure in human subjects. This line of research led to his discovering that transcendental meditation could lower the pressure increased by environmental stress. This line of research was later applied to insomnia, irregular heartbeats, angina pectoris, premenstrual syndrome (PMS), infertility, and even depression.

Benson and his team began looking at how the expectation of whether or not medication for depression would work. Diederich and Goetz (2008) studied the availability of serotonin (an essential neurotransmitter for mood regulation) in the "placebo effect" in recovery from depression. They also found out through neuroimaging methods that the placebo effect created changes in the frontal and cingulate cortical activity. This study reports that up to 50 percent of depression patients can be helped with depression symptoms through expectation of being helped. Benson (2010) concludes that healing of depression depends on accessing the power of inner convictions and "anticipation that a particular therapeutic activity will actually lead to improvement of health."

In his more recent book *Relaxation Revolution* (2010), Benson develops a two-phased procedure: relaxation response trigger and visualization. The purpose of the relaxation trigger is to accomplish a physiological state including healthier metabolism, lower blood pressure, slower heart and breathing rates, and "an overall calming of the brain, and a sense of relaxation and well-being." His research suggests that when you have developed this level of relaxation, there will also be healthier expression of genes.

There are numerous ways of arriving at this relaxed state of mind and body. The method used in many of the studies conducted at Harvard University seems to be drawn from Eastern meditation procedures:

Step 1. Pick a "mantra" or focus word(s), image, or your breathing. It is interesting from the perspective of this book that a "short prayer" is also included. Whatever words you choose should be emotionally calming and in accord with your deepest beliefs. We are eventually going to suggest that the practice of the repetition of the psalms has done this for centuries.

Step 2. Find a quiet place where there is little likelihood that you will be disturbed. By all means, turn off your cell phone. Our experience is that this must be done away from home due to children, telephone calls, and well-meaning family members interrupting. This could be in a grotto, out in the woods, in an open church, etc.

Step 3. Close your eyes. This means that you have to be in a "safe" place so that your limbic system can relax and release from survival mode. The "focus" must be on your internal world (the words or images you produce), not on the external world that triggers the activation of the limbic system.

Step 4. For the first few minutes with eyes closed, you need to eliminate the body tension by relaxing your body. Slowly go from toes, feet, legs, abdomen, back, shoulders, neck, and face. Mentally focus sequentially on these body parts, attempting to relax the muscles in each of those parts.

Step 5. Now try to breathe slowly and naturally. As you exhale, begin repeating the word(s), prayer, or image that you have chosen. If you have chosen breathing, focus on your breathing rhythm. It seems to help to sit erectly on a chair, church pew, bench, or do the lotus position with legs crossed on the ground or floor.

Step 6. Try to keep a don't-care attitude. Make sure that you are not thinking about the past or the future. Don't even care about how well you are keeping these steps. The goal of this is to change the physiological state from concern about the responsibilities, past and future, to a state of present relaxation. It is very hard to let go of the normal stressors in your life where no fear or concern exists. If you come out of a background of insecure attachment or trauma, it is quite hard to put yourself into this relaxed state of mind and body. If distracting thoughts burst into your consciousness, calmly focus on the word, prayer, or breathing. If there is a great deal of stress in your current life, you may find frequent distractions in the beginning. Due to the quiet state that you are attempting to create, you may also find that you are more aware of body aches and pains. This will pass if you just refocus on your mantra.

Step 7. Although you may not be able to do so at first try, get this initial meditation period up to twelve to fifteen minutes daily. You will not get the health and calming benefits from meditation unless you do it for this recommended range.

Step 8. Find a time of day when you can daily meditate. Getting up early in the morning before breakfast works best for many, but the most important issue is that you find a time each day to meditate. You will need to make a commitment to meditate each day for about fifteen minutes for thirty days. According to Benson and Proctor (2010), this is about how long it takes to develop a habit. This also is about how long it takes to really form brain circuits releasing opioids and dopamine in the reward center of the brain. Once that occurs, you will want to keep up meditation because it makes you feel better (Benson and Proctor 2010).

Benson and his researchers, as suggested in the preface, claim that this relaxation response can be elicited also through aerobic exercise, repetitive prayer, progressive muscle relaxation, playing a musical instrument or singing, listening to music, and engaging in tasks that require "mindless repetitive movements." We will now discuss each of these methods.

Aerobic exercise has been associated with good health in numerous studies over the years. Jensen (2008) has stated that all the things one can do for a healthy brain aerobic exercise is the most important. In a recent meta-analysis of studies on brain-based interventions exercise, especially for aging brains, aerobic exercise was also one of the best-documented procedures. One of the main reasons for this phenomenon is that when the heart is pumping more rapidly, each neuron in the brain receives more oxygen and other nutrients needed for efficient functioning. Such exercise may also increase the production of the nerve growth factor (NGF), a hormone that enhances brain functioning. Most importantly, repetitive exercise stimulates the production of dopamine (the feel-good neurotransmitter). New neurons can also be generated through repetitive exercise, especially in the hippocampal areas of the brain, improving memory processes (Jensen 2008). Also, endorphins (chemicals in the brain that produce a calming effect) are stimulated in aerobic exercise (Somer 1999). People often report this calming experience right after finishing fifteen-plus minutes of this kind of exercise—"runner's high." On the other hand, exercises that require short bursts of high energy and concentration on playmaking do not seem to produce the same sense of "relaxation." Running, bicycling, aerobic dance, and swimming work; but basketball, tennis, golf, baseball, and football do not. The latter may be good for your body conditioning, but they do not stimulate the relaxation response.

Repetitive prayer can also stimulate the relaxation response. Especially in Western religions, repeating words and phrases—such as praying the rosary and reading the Bible or other revered written texts—is common practice. What seems to be common in Eastern and Western meditation is the "repetition" in an almost "mindless" state. In ritualistic prayer, the content is not as important as the underlying belief and repetition of a word(s). Benson and Proctor (2010) even suggest that "you remind yourself that you really do believe in the particular repetitive prayer you are using." We will later follow up on this idea with a chapter on prayer.

Progressive muscle relaxation is also useful learning to relax. We have known for many years that relaxing the muscles throughout the body helps calm the mind. Muscle relaxation has been used for many years in the treatment of anxiety problems such as panic disorder (Craske and Barlow 2008). The actual exercises instruct a patient to tense a muscle group, such as the hands, for about ten seconds and then relaxing the muscles for fifteen seconds while paying attention to the relaxing experience. You are instructed to do this exercise sequentially throughout your body: fists, biceps, triceps, forehead muscles, muscles around the eyes, jaw muscles, neck muscles, shoulders, chest, stomach, lower back, buttocks, thighs, calf muscles, and feet. At the end of the progressive relaxation, you are instructed to attend to the experience of a wave of relaxation spreading throughout your body (Bourne 1995).

Music—whether listened to, played on a musical instrument, or sung—is another important way that man calms down the brain and experiences the relaxation response according the research of Benson and Proctor (2010). The brain has evolved to be especially sensitive to musical sounds. Weinberger (1995) reports research that backs the hypothesis that the auditory cortex responds to pitch and tones and that individual neurons process melodic contour. Clynes (1982) suggests that music engages the whole brain. We also know from past research that music increases muscular and molecular energy. It also influences the rate of our heartbeat and can alter metabolism. The reason that music is often played in hospital and health-care offices is that music can reduce pain and stress and speeds up healing and recovery after surgery. It can also relieve fatigue. No wonder so many people play music as they are coming home from work (Jensen 2000).

Music stimulates the limbic system, so critical in emotional processing as mentioned earlier. It increases arousal for good or bad. The cell phone to the ear may stimulate socially appropriate or inappropriate behavior. If adolescents act before thinking, some music is certainly able to stimulate aggressive and sexual acting out. On the other hand, liturgical music is capable of keeping our mind aroused and focused on our relationship with God. So it is no wonder that Benson and Proctor (2010) found that listening to or producing music stimulates the relaxation response and calms the anxious brain.

"Mindless" repetitive movements (Benson and Proctor 2010) also have the potential to make us feel relaxed: doodling, knitting, gardening, etc. Sometimes just watching or hearing repetitive movements or sounds can clam us down. When I was studying at the University of Maine, I would go to a park

that bordered the Atlantic Ocean. I could sit on the edge of a granite cliff and watch the tide smash against the cliff far below. The rhythmic sounds and view of wave after wave put me in a very relaxed state of mind. Anticipatory fears and anxieties were far from my mind. If I were insecurely attached, I might be sitting there thinking of how no one really cared about me, even if I fell into the ocean in a very anxious state of mind, and would have trouble keeping my mind on the sights and sounds of the ocean. Once again, I can only be thankful that my parents cared for me well in early infancy so that I could cherish the moment and see the lobster boats dancing rhythmically to the beat of the ocean.

Although eliciting that the relaxation response in any of the above means according to Benson and Proctor (2010) will lead to significant healing of the mind and body, they found out that to increase the chances of living a healthier life, *visualization* also needs to be practiced. There is a long history of research on the use of visualization or imagination in getting better control over one's life. Focusing on calming and relaxing mental imagery will increase your ability to live a life that is healthier and happier.

After you have spent twelve to fifteen minutes relaxing yourself through meditation, prayer, exercise, listening to music, etc., you are prepared to use the Benson visualization exercise. To do so, close your eyes and see yourself in a healthy state. If you are someone who is coping with back pain, see yourself as running and jumping with no pain. In the context of this book, see yourself as not having a care in the world, as happy and carefree—perhaps as a child running outside, picking flowers, and doing somersaults. In this exercise, see yourself and relive a period of time when you were well and happy. Recall a time when you were symptom-free. Recall and imagine what it would feel like to not feel depressed or anxious. Relive a state of wellness from the past. Even if you have no memory of such a time, imagine what it would be like to be carefree and happy.

The main ideas of the visualization exercise are to identify your particular disease or unhealthy state of mind and to see yourself without that symptom or disease. In our context, visualize yourself under extreme stress from some realistic situation but able to handle it without fear or anxiety. As mentioned earlier, relationally traumatized individuals have very poor ability to handle age appropriate stresses of life. If you are a mother who gets angry, yells, and hits your children when they misbehave, visualize yourself in that situation calmly talking to your children and setting boundaries to handle the situation. Then let yourself feel the satisfaction of being a good mother, without anxiety or guilt for getting out of control.

The research of Benson and Proctor (2010) suggests that you need to do this visualization exercise for about eight to ten minutes. Play with the situation in your imagination, varying the situation but always coming back to see yourself as free of the symptoms, whether it be an aching back or anxiety. At the end of the ten minutes, keep your eyes closed but slowly let "normal" thoughts back into your mind. Then open your eyes and sit for another minute quietly.

Numerous studies using neuroimaging have verified that when the relaxation response is stimulated, the executive control areas of the brain (frontal lobe) are activated with resulting improvement in attention and concentration. "Their brain became calmer and more open to new thoughts" (Benson and Proctor 2010). Further research has indicated that "remembered wellness" is also part of the success story. Remembered wellness occurs when a patient wills the belief and expectation to occur. If, day after day, you visualize yourself without pain and anxiety, you can slowly restructure your expectations of good health rather than bad—from the expectation of pain and anxiety to the expectation of a healthy body and mind. This expectation is crucial in the insecurely attached. If you expect that others will not care about or for you, you will do things that will make the expectation come true. You will do obnoxious things that will incline others to reject you: lying, stealing, pushiness, etc. If, on the other hand, you repeatedly see yourself as loveable and worthy of care, you will slowly be more confident and do things that are appealing to your friends or spouse. You are now calmer and more confident. The Benson protocol is a very powerful means of going from insecure to secure, from depression and anxiety to a healthier mind and body.

6

The Body of Christ and Our Synaptic Connection

AT THIS POINT, WE NEED to go back and look at the brain as social. The brain is composed of trillions of connections through neurons and dendrites as explained in chapter 2. For the body to move, think, and act, information has to be able to flow back and forward through these many intricate connections. The brain continues to form new patterns and networks primarily through interactions with other individuals and groups. The human brain has evolved to interact with others. If we were securely attached in infancy, we slowly develop social networks to understand, predict, and adapt to others. If we have not had a satisfactory relationship early in life, the connections between the limbic system and the frontal areas of the brain are not well developed. As a result, we become socially impaired: not understanding others, not predicting their behavior well, and not adapting socially.

Yet the world is composed of some individuals who have socially healthy brains and others who do not. If Ainsworth's (1978) research is correct, about 40 percent are at risk to have poorly adapted brains and 60 percent healthy ones. My clinical impression is that individuals are distributed over a continuum of attachment security. Some of the insecurely attached do get better due to later relationships, but that is not the majority. We have to find a way to live together without fear and aggression. As we all know, this has not always happened.

The relationship between God and man, as recorded in the sacred scriptures, depicts a loving God who creates man and forms a covenant (testament) or contract with man that He will be their God, protecting them and caring for them.

The covenant with Abraham is more of a promise of land, many descendants and a special relationship between his descendants and God. It is interesting that God is depicted as asking nothing back form Abraham and his descendants. Contrariwise, the Mosaic covenant with the Hebrews at Mount Sinai promises security and protection but is conditioned on the Hebrews' fidelity in keeping the commandments. The laws are divinely ordained, and violations are now "sins." The

Davidic covenant promises political stability, secure worship in the temple, but no conditions on the descendants' part.

The similarity between this relationship and the attachment relationship between primary caretaker and infant is quite clear. The dialogue between God and Job could have been between a mother or father and their son over finances for college education. This is why Granqvist and Kirkpatrick (2008) and others see the relationship between God and man as fulfilling the characteristics of an attachment relationship.

In the New Testament, we see that the covenant between God and man is extended not only to the Jewish descendants but to all people who believe that Christ, the Son of God, is their Savior, the one who provides security and survival. Throughout the New Testament, we see analogies and metaphors used in which God cares for His people—whether diseased, possessed by the devil, or sinners who have chosen selfish motives over the covenant with God. Christ is pictured as caring for all of them lest they do not survive. This is always the fear of man—survival. This is what we are always anxious about: not having enough money, housing, or food to survive. God promised His people that they would survive for all eternity if they trusted in Him and kept his rules (commandments). Even when they broke his rules, He would forgive them as long as they remained committed to Him. Christ quotes Jeremiah (31:31–34) in Hebrews (8:6–13), ending the Old Testament and establishing the New Testament through the shedding of His blood.

At the Last Supper, Christ is quoted by Matthew (26:27): "He took a cup, and when he had given thanks he handed it to them saying, 'Drink from this, all of you, for this is my blood, the blood of the covenant, poured out for many for the forgiveness of sins.'"

St. Paul has followed this up by saying that, through the church, we all are attached to God because through faith and baptism (commitment to Christ), we become one with Christ. It is significant that in St. Paul's conversion, we hear Jesus addressing him, saying, "Saul, Saul, why are you persecuting me?" He does not say, "Why are you persecuting my followers?" He explains this further in 1 Corinthians 12:12–16:

> For as with the human body which is a unity although it has many parts—all the parts of. the body, though many, still making up one single body—so it is with Christ. We were baptized into one body in a single Spirit, Jews as well as Greeks, slaves as well as free men, and we were all given the same Spirit. And indeed the body consists not of one member but many. If the foot were to say, "I am not a hand and so do not belong to the body," it does not belong to the body any the less for that. Or if the ear were to say, "I am not an eye, and so I do not belong to the body," that would not stop its belonging to the body.

Although, some have interpreted these texts as an analogy to emphasize unity and not a reality (Shults 2002) and have questioned who the members are. It has been called "mystical" because it is not easy to understand how we are the body of Christ, as St. Paul clearly asserts, and at the same time believe in the resurrection of Christ. For our discussion here, we will accept St. Paul's words as reality, not analogy.

In continued reading of St. Paul, it becomes clear that he believed that through baptism, we become Christ. "Now Christ's body is yourselves, each of you with a part to play in the whole" (1 Cor. 8:27). Just as the ear and hand play different roles in the human body, so each of us are assigned roles: apostles, prophets, teachers, healers, and helpers. Above all, we must love the other parts. Love is the glue that binds us together in this mystical body, Christ. Love is patient and kind—not jealous, boastful, or conceited. "It is always ready to make allowances, to trust, to hope and to endure whatever comes" (1 Cor. 13: 7).

This is a pretty good description of the securely attached who learned intimacy and the capacity to love from their mothers and fathers who cared for them. Also remember what Colozino (2010) said about the social brain and attachment to groups. We use the same attachment strategies to relate to groups as individuals. The body of Christ is composed of many different parts. Some are very securely attached, others very insecurely. Because we are all baptized into Christ, we have very different capacity to love and care for one another. When we have an infected part in our physical bodies, blood cells rush to the site to attack the bacteria to heal the hand so that it can do its assigned function.

If we are attached to God through Christ, we will not have to worry about survival. The analogy of the shepherd who cares for each of his sheep to the extent that he will search for anyone who is missing is central to the message of Christ. If I am insecurely attached, harboring the eternal doubt that anyone cares about me, it is very consoling to realize that I am a part of something very profound, Christ Himself. Christ is the head of the body who cares about all the members as a shepherd cares for his sheep. Through mindfulness and prayer, we will learn how to keep this realization central to our awareness.

7

Mindfulness

THERE IS A GROWING BODY of literature and research on "mindfulness" that seems almost contrary to psychology and psychiatry's self-definition of being scientific. For it is primarily experiential.

Mindfulness is the ability to focus on the present by improving attention. Most of us can remember arriving at a destination without knowing how we got there or reading a page without knowing what you read. In conversation, you might suddenly become aware that someone is speaking to you, but you have no ideas what they have said to you. In these experiences, attention to the moment has failed. It is likely that you were thinking of something else in the future or past and missed the present. If you have an anxious mind, you often are living in the past or future and miss the experience of the moment. You need to learn to *be* in the present. This is precisely why mindfulness and meditation calm the anxious mind.

Shapiro and Carlson (2009) suggest that it is both an awareness and a process. They define *mindfulness* as "an awareness that arises through intentionally attending in an open, caring, and nonjudgmental way." Jon Kabat-Zinn (1994) gives a simple definition: "Mindfulness means paying attention in a particular way: on purpose, in the present moment and nonjudgmentally."

Kubat-Zinn's work—according to Segal, Williams, and Teasdale (2002)—has been integrated into medical treatment of a variety of physical illnesses at the University of Massachusetts Medical Center. This, of course, is not surprising in that Benson (2010) had been doing similar treatment there (mentioned earlier in chapter 5) under the concept of the relaxation response.

Mindfulness is knowing your state of mind, both cognitively and emotionally, "without judging it, evaluating it, thinking about it, or trying to change it" (Shapiro and Carlson 2010). Mindfulness is an awareness of each moment as it arises and passes away. It is a way of relating to all experiences of life in an open and accepting manner. It does not want the experience to be different. Our current reality is generated by our present perception and judgment about it.

This understanding of "mindfulness" is heavily dependent on Eastern and Buddhist scholars.

Thirty-five years ago, Jon Kabat-Zinn developed an eight-week stress-reduction program called mindfulness-based stress reduction (MBSR). At the time, he was a pioneer in bringing Eastern thought into the Western world and applying it to medical conditions. He reports that it is not a technical trick but a way of being. In an interview, Kabat-Zenn states, "I have a lot of faith that if people just learn to be in the present through simple mindfulness meditation, then the practice does the work of transformation and Healing" (Boyce 2014).

A fundamental process in mindfulness is being able to "reperceive" the experience of self. One has to be able to look at conscious experiences nonjudgmentally. Then you are not embedded with your fears and anxieties. You are with the fears, not defined by them. Mindfulness allows you to be with your thoughts and emotions rather than being defined by them. A person learns to stand back from his experiences (pain, depression, anger, or other emotions) and live with them without needing to defend against them. The insecurely attached, as mentioned earlier, have poorly developed egos that are always worrying about survival. They cannot accept that they are "lovable" and worthy of care. In a mindful state, the survival fears are just perceived as being there without the need to control. The circular doubt about being worthy of love just does not matter in that state of mind.

Mindfulness has become more and more a legitimate therapeutic intervention. The use of mindfulness helps the patient learn to experience the "here and now" in the hour of therapy. Ogden (2009) points out that the patient and therapist together learn how to perceive how experiences can be managed and expanded. Difficult thoughts and emotions don't need to be controlled or eradicated but only accepted as part of the present experience. We will pick up this procedure again in talking about prayer and the experience of God.

The *Mindful Way Workbook* (Teasdale et al. 2014) lists eight themes spread over eight weeks of change in learning to meditate:

- Week 1: Moving from living on "automatic pilot" to living with awareness and conscious choice
- Week 2: Moving from relating to experience through thinking to directly sensing
- Week 3: Moving from dwelling in the past and future to being fully in the present moment
- Week 4: Moving from trying to avoid, escape, or get rid of unpleasant experiences to approaching it with interest
- Week 5: Moving from needing things to be different to allowing them to be just as they already are
- Week 6: Moving from seeing thoughts as true and real to seeing them as mental events that may not correspond to reality

- Week 7: Moving from treating yourself harshly to taking care of yourself with kindness and compassion
- Week 8: Planning a mindful future

A basic principle of mindfulness expressed by Shapiro and Carlson (2010) is that "intentionally cultivating nonjudgmental attention leads to connection, which leads to self-regulation and ultimately to greater order and health." We began by suggesting that infants who are exposed to neglect and abuse during the first year of life develop brains with poor capacity to regulate emotions. So we are now suggesting that one way of changing their brains is through reperceiving their experiences and living in the here and now without the need to control those around them. Their survival fear is just there without the need to react or escape. Recent research has indicated that attention skills, interpersonal relationships and happiness in marriage, self-concept, increases in positive affect, self-compassion, and empathy are improved with learning how to experience the present more deeply (Shapiro and Carlson 2010). Is it not interesting that all these areas are deficits in individuals with histories of neglect and abuse? In summary, we have very good reason to further investigate how mindfulness is practiced in Eastern and Western cultures.

Amishi P. Jha (2013) quotes Scott Rogers, the director of Programs and Training, Mindfulness Research and Practice initiative at the University of Miami, in giving us a sample of a ten- to fifteen-minute mindfulness exercise:

- Sit in an upright position, hands resting on your thighs or cradled together.
- Lower or close your eyes, whichever is more comfortable for you.
- Attend to your breath, following its movement throughout your body.
- Notice the sensations around your belly as air flows into and out of your nose or mouth. You have been breathing all day—all of your life—and in this moment, you are simply noticing your breath.
- Select one area of your body affected by your breathing and focus your attention there. Control your focus, not the breathing itself.
- When you notice your mind wandering—and it will—bring your attention back to your breath.
- After five to ten minutes, switch from focusing to monitoring. Think of your mind as a vast open sky; and your thoughts, feelings, and sensations as passing clouds.
- Feel your whole body move with your breath. Be receptive to your sensations, noticing what arises in the moment. Be attentive to the changing quality of experience—sounds, aromas, the caress of a breeze—thoughts.
- After about five more minutes, lift your gaze or open your eyes.

The above instructions are quite clearly an adaptation of Eastern meditation procedures. In chapter 8, we will follow up with a better understanding of Eastern and Western meditation.

Herbert Benson (2010) sees the need and practice of mindfulness as a "revolution." It appears to be the latest cult in health psychology and find its application in penitentiary treatment and, of all places, the world of business.

David's Penitentiary Stay

David continued to steal from home and in the community. David did not finish high school and found every reason not to complete job applications. Mel and Lea were very frustrated over this and did not know what to do. One day, David was just gone. He lived on the street and quickly began selling street drugs to supply his own drug habit and to survive. Even in the drug world, he did not fit in. He tried cheating drug lords and nearly escaped with his life by contacting Mel to cool his heels at home for a few weeks. Then he disappeared again. His lack of intimacy skills left him as a loner among the antisocial underworld.

Because of what happened in the drug world, he switched to weapons. He went to farmers' houses and knocked on the door. If someone answered, he would ask for directions. If no one answered, he would break in and steal whatever he found. Often it was guns. He slowly became the supplier of weapons for gang members in Omaha. The police gang squad soon became aware of his role in supplying guns. Soon David caught on and knew that his freedom would soon end. This was shortly after the infamous white bronco ride of O. J. Simpson. David stole a white bronco and was driving it down Dodge Street when the police caught up with him. They threw down rolls of spikes that blew out the tires on the bronco. The capture was recorded on the TV news stations. Mel always thought that David called the media to show dramatically his capture. His need for attention finally realized in an exaggerated fashion.

David was facing a forty-year penitentiary sentence. At the time of sentencing, the judge said, "What do you have to say for yourself, young man?" David replied, "Your Honor, I was in a very high-class psychiatric hospital where I was diagnosed with bipolar disorder and placed on lithium. But I have been very poor lately and could not buy the lithium. When I committed the robberies and stole the bronco, I was in a manic state and did not really know what I was doing. Please have mercy on me." The judge did just that and reduced the sentence to twelve years. David was always at his best when attempting to squirm out of the consequences of his antisocial behavior.

Because David was a "loner," he did pretty bad time in the penitentiary. He hated it there due to the loss of control. His anger only made his time tougher. And then a wonderful thing happened. David met Fr. Joel Lund, an Episcopal priest who was working among the prisoners at the time. David initially only wanted attention and time alone with Fr. Joel, safe from the dangers of penitentiary life. In the beginning, Joel just gave him the attention and importance that he wanted. Soon he began working with David's fears and anxieties. David had been taught about God through his adoptive parents, and he had been baptized as a Christian. Fr. Joel used this hook to work on his belief system. More and more, they worked on David's need for safety and security. David really liked the theme of God as the Good Shepherd. Eventually the relationship with God included communicating with God through prayer and meditation. David certainly had plenty of time to learn how to meditate as a Christian. It did not take too long before David got better and better at accepting the present reality without judging himself or the penitentiary personnel. It surprised David how doing his time seemed to change.

After six years in the penitentiary, he was released on "good time." He got a job in a used-furniture store and eventually was promoted to running the store. One day, an attractive young woman came in the store with her three children to look at furniture. To make a long story short, they eventually married and are raising the three children as their own. Recently, David contacted me, and I visited him and his family far away from Omaha. I could hardly believe how changed David was. There was a calmness about him, and for the first time, he seemed happy with life. I doubt that I had much to do with his serenity, but it was such a delight to see an honest smile spread across his face as I shook his hand. There is a God who cares for each of us, even if the journey is a bit crooked.

8

Christian Meditation

MINDFULNESS, AS WAY OF BEING, is certainly rooted in Eastern meditation. Meditation in some form has been practiced since as early as 1500 BC. The Buddhist practiced meditation as early as the fourth century BC (Everly and Lating, 2002). In the West in 20 BC, Philo of Alexandria wrote of "spiritual exercises" involving "attention" and "concentration." By the third century AD, Plotinus developed some form of meditation (Hadot and Davidson, 1995). St. Augustine experimented with it unsuccessfully (von Balthasar, 1989).

There is some evidence that meditation was always practiced in Judaism (Joshua 1:8).

Early Christian meditation seems to go back to the early church and—by the Middle Ages, especially in the Byzantine era—to have borrowed some techniques of meditation from Eastern meditation. Between the tenth and fourteenth centuries, it involved some form of "mantra" to be repeated. Eventually Western Christian meditation involved a "ladder" described by the Benedictine monk Guigo II with the Latin terms *lectio, meditatio, oratio, and contemplatio* (read, meditate, pray, and contemplate) (Wortley, 2006).

The Congregation for the Doctrine of Faith (the Catholic Curia) in 1989, in the letter "Orationis formas"(1989), warned of the fundamental error of combining Christian and non-Christian forms of meditation. Nonetheless, Christian meditation has continued to show influences of learning how to communicate with God in a here-and-now manner.

If we look at the history of Christian monasticism, we are led to the third century AD when a group of men and women retreated to the desert, likely stimulated by the persecution of Diocletian in the beginning of the third century. These early Christians formed an alternative way of life. Anthony the Great spearheaded this movement. He viewed solidarity as a way to "focus one's attention on refining and purifying the spirit" (Cunningham and Egan, 1996). Under the inspiration of Anthony, groups of both men and women retreated to the desert and began practicing an extreme form of asceticism. They left the pleasures of the world and began a contemplative lifestyle of praying the psalms. These groups of early monastics eventually were called the Desert Fathers.

One of the components of the monastic life in the desert was "melete." There was some controversy over the meaning of this word. The translation from Greek to Latin to English ended up with the word *meditation*. Yet it probably was anything but quiet. It amounted to the recitation of the psalms to protect oneself from the temptations of the world. Most of the time, these psalms were repeated by memory as one does their work and were generally sung (Wortley 2006).

Both Eastern and Western Christian meditation seem to have taken their origins from the Desert Fathers. In the West, there was progression of the singing of the psalms through monastic orders, especially the Benedictines. The monk Guigo II in the twelfth century summarized their way of life: lectio, meditatio, oratio, and contemplatio (read, ponder, pray, contemplate (Egan, 1991). They took reading from scripture, especially the psalms, and repeated them throughout the day. What one suspects is that they were able, through repetition of these readings, to put their attention on some attribute of God and block out all other thoughts. When outside thoughts came, they were able to look at them as "from the outside" and attend to their feelings about them in their relation to God. St. John of the Cross—mystic, poet, and artist—was able to mentally withdraw into the experience of God "to remain alone in the loving awareness of God" (Kavanaugh and Rodriguez 1991).

What seems common between the contemplatives and Western meditators is the desire to be united to Christ. One form of meditation is to sit at his feet and wait in his presence, just like the child who sits in his mother or father's lap to be comforted (von Balthasar, 1989). Potential meditators are directed to find a "quiet place" with the sounds of nature and the like and to focus on a scriptural mantra such as "the Lord is my Shepherd."

Attachment theory suggests that the infant's whole attention is on the mother, waiting to be cared for in order to survive. The eye-to-eye gazing and reciprocal verbalizations are explained earlier under the concept of "intimacy." It is this attention and adoration of the attachment object (primary caregiver) that tends to get lost as we become more self-absorbed. But we do see it in lovers as they report gazing at each other. This language of lovers is renewed through the praying of the psalms.

Contemplative prayer has been described as picking a short scripture passage and then reflecting on it for hours or the whole day. Christians who practiced contemplative prayer made the passage their own by measuring their life and behavior. They contemplated what this scripture meant to their life personally. In this manner, they became more and more absorbed into Christ, more unified and identified with Christ.

When I was in the novitiate (spiritual training year) for the Society of the Precious Blood, every hour on the first minute of the hour, the oldest cleric in group would say, "Let us place ourselves in the presence of God." For just one minute, we would again sense that God was present in silence. Then we would go back to the lawn mower or baseball bat with the sense that whatever we were doing was related to a much bigger and eternal being. It was a way of getting our priorities clear. The priority of getting the lawn cut or hitting a home run was entirely different when you saw yourself in the presence of God in nature around you. The "awe" in the presence of God is a very calming perception.

We originally said that our brains are affected by the early nurturance and experience of trauma. If attachment was insecure, we have a much harder time managing impulses and regulating emotions and relating to others. In working as a psychologist for many years with people from infancy to old age, it is my conviction that people can be placed on a continuum of attachment. Some people worry not at all about whether they are loved or cared for, and others worry about it all the time. The hyperactive limbic system and poorly wired frontal lobe leave the insecurely attached with some level of tension and anxiety in their day-to-day activities that either inclines others to approve or disapprove. When others evaluate us at work or play, we are all somewhat uneasy. We want to be respected and cared for by others. We don't know 100 percent whether someone really loves us even when they say so. We believe that prayer and contemplation is a way of putting ourselves in a healthier perspective. This is why we saw earlier that people with religious or spiritual beliefs were happier and had fewer anxieties and depressed states.

Neuroscientists have been studying what happens in the brain when individuals meditate. Brain circuits that have been identified are the occipital parietal (concrete images in children), parietal-frontal (relationship between you and God), frontal lobe (creates and integrates and predicts your future relationship with God), thalamus (makes God feel "real" and integrates ideas about God), amygdala (gives emotional valence to the concept of God, both positive and negative), striatum (inhibits fear in the amygdala and allows you to feel safe in God's presence) (Newberg and Waldman 2010).

A large number of scientific studies have documented that meditation decreases oxygen consumption, respiration rate, heart rate, and blood pressure. These studies and others led Benson (2010) to look at the value of meditation on physical health problems such as cancer and cardiac disorders. We have already discussed his work in an earlier chapter.

This is perhaps what Maslow was realizing in suggesting that we do have a higher need for spirituality at the peak of the need hierarchy (Maslow 1962). It is interesting to note the similarity of qualities in the "self-actualized" person and individuals who meditate on a regular basis. Maslow (1962) lists the following characteristics:

1. Superior perception of reality
2. Increased acceptance of self, of others, and of nature
3. Increased spontaneity

4. Increase in problem centering.
5. Increased detachment and desire for privacy
6. Increased autonomy and resistance to enculturation
7. Greater freshness of appreciation and richness of emotional reaction
8. Higher frequency of peak experiences
9. Increased identification with the human species
10. Changed (the clinician would say "improved") interpersonal relations
11. More democratic character structure
12. Greatly increased creativeness
13. Certain changes in the value system

It is my impression that the above list is found in healthy relaxed brains of individuals who have found out how to *be* rather than *become*. In a religious or spiritual context, it means that they have learned how to be in the presence of God rather than worrying about becoming something in the future. Unfortunately, Western thought and religions have inclined us to become rather be. Attachment theory suggests that infants who are securely attached experience satisfaction and safety *being* with the attached object (parent). Because attachment security is not always secure, many individuals struggle with attachment-related anxiety. This can be recovered through accepting new safe attachment objects (Hughes 2013).

Our brains seem to be designed for spiritual experiences and satisfaction (D'Aquili and Newberg 1999). This, of course, is the neurological correlate of Maslow's (1962) "peak experiences."

9

Relaxation Through Praying the Psalms

ALTHOUGH THERE ARE AT LEAST twenty references to meditation in the Bible (Newberg and Waldman 2010), most people are not aware of the use of meditation in the scriptures. In Joshua (1:8), we read, "Have the book of this law always on your lips; meditate on it day and night so that you may carefully keep everything that is written in it." In the Jerusalem Bible (1966), the Psalms frequently use the word *ponder* or *think about* when referring to the precepts and words of the Lord. As a result, the book of Psalms was prayed by the Hebrew people for centuries before the birth of

Christ (Bamburger 1981). A major part of Jewish liturgy was praying the psalms in the temple and later in the synagogues. Much of the worship and "spirit" of the Jews were formed through the praying of the psalms or the pondering of the psalms. We can be quite sure that Mary, Joseph, Elizabeth, Zachary, John the Baptist, and Christ himself prayed and meditated on the psalms.

In the early years of the church, this tradition was continued. There are some 116 citations of the book of Psalms in the New Testament (Bamburger 1981). As the early liturgies developed in the church, the psalms were the basis of prayer and education on the spiritual life.

The importance of praying and meditating on the psalms continued up until the Reformation. After the Reformation, the Catholic tradition minimized the use of scripture in teaching and instead emphasized the teaching authority of the church's magisterium. Just the opposite was true in the Protestant tradition. But this was not so in the monasteries of the Catholic Church where praying the Divine Office, composed primarily in repetition of the psalms, was preserved. The psalter gradually became the prayer of monks, nuns, and the clergy. The vast majority of the laity prayed in nonliturgical and nonbiblical forms. Vatican II attempted to turn this trend back to the traditional liturgical, scripture-based praying of the psalms. One of the means of doing this was to put the scripture-based liturgy in the vernacular instead of the "dead" language of Latin. For many centuries, only priests and monks knew the Latin language.

A very important trend was to try to get nonclerics to pray using the psalms again. In the 1970s, Friar Thomas Keating (1994) adjusted the centuries-long manner of meditating the psalms, calling it the *centering prayer*. This method brings us into a contemplative attitude of "listening and receptivity." He saw it as a preparation for contemplation through reducing the obstacles caused by the "hyperactivity of our minds and our lives." It is this very hyperactivity of the limbic system, along with the impairment of the orbital frontal lobe (Schore 2003), which we have described in an earlier chapter, that we now find Keating suggesting a meditative state as a remedy.

Keating (1994) further explains these methods by saying that you pick a word from scripture and focus on it for twenty minutes or longer with your eyes closed. When distracting thoughts come to you, just return your mind to the focus word.

Thomas Merton (1969) believed that contemplation and meditation, as he understood it, was not just for monks but for all Christians who face the distractions and stresses of modern, urban life in order to "keep themselves together, to maintain their human and Christian identity and their spiritual freedom." Merton describes the "prayer of the heart" as interior recollection, abandoning distractions, and "humble invocation of the Lord Jesus with words from the Bible in a spirit of intense faith." He asserts that meditation and contemplative prayer is "not so much a way to find God as a way of resting in him whom we have found." Learning just to be with God rather than becoming someone for God (mentioned earlier) is part of the "prayer of the heart." This involves a totally wordless and total "surrender of the heart" in silence. Adolescents who are stuck in a self-serving narcissism often report that they cannot stand silence. This may be due to the fact that they cannot accept their own confrontation with "self."

Until each individual comes to term with self as dependent on a higher reality for survival, silence is intolerable. If so, perhaps contemplative prayer is the means to letting go of "selfish" demands to be at peace with the presence of God.

In the process of letting go of "worldly" demands and wants, the contemplative must be ready for what St. John of the Cross (Kavanaugh and Rodriguez 1991) described as the "dark night of the soul"—where their own wishes, their self-esteem, "their presumption, their aggressivity... are systematically humiliated." Only when the narcissistic attitude is purged and filled instead with a "higher and purer" capacity to experience God do we come to contemplation (Merton 1969).

In the first letter to the Thessalonians (1 Thess. 5, 16–18), St. Paul writes, "Always be joyful; pray constantly; and for all things give thanks; this is the will of God for you in Christ Jesus." It was this admonition that led the Desert Fathers to form the roots of praying throughout the day, leading to the eventual development of the recitation of the Divine Office.

As mentioned earlier, in order to get the whole church to participate in this continuous prayer, Vatican II simplified these prayers and permitted them to be done in the vernacular. The resulting book of prayer is called the *Christian Prayer: The Liturgy of the Hours* (1976) and is prayed by monks, nuns, and the laity throughout the world. The book is divided into four times of praying: morning, daytime, evening, and night. This follows the cry of David in Psalm 55:17: "Evening, morning and at noon I will cry and lament." In each time interval, scriptural readings and recitation of the psalms are done. In monasteries, the psalms are sung in Gregorian chant. In this manner, the church is fulfilling the mandate of St. Paul to pray constantly. For some people, this is the way of staying "focused" on God and having a contemplative spirit. If your sincere faith allows you to participate in the Christian prayer, it will allow you to be a calmer, more peaceful person. As we have tried to document, it will calm down your brain so that you can lead a healthier, more peaceful life.

Much of the research on mindfulness and meditation as a means of calming the brain has been done with Eastern meditation techniques. It is important to note that Eastern and Western meditation are very similar. One of the more powerful pieces of research in this matter was done by Newberg (2010). In 1999, he studied a group of nuns who had been practicing the centering prayer of Keating. This was the first brain-scan study of Christian meditation and contemplation. Two findings came out of this study: the meditating nuns' brains looked very different from normal human brains at rest, and the neurological changes were very similar to Buddhist monks when meditating. Even though the religious beliefs that motivated the meditation were very different, the meditating brains looked very similar. What were common in both are "ritual techniques of breathing, staying relaxed, and focusing one's attention upon a concept that evokes comfort, compassion, or a spiritual sense of peace" (Newberg and Waldman 2010). The final conclusion of this line of research is that one would expect that Christian meditation, as described by Keating, would have the same calming potential as Eastern meditation, which has been more thoroughly researched under the concept of "mindfulness" and "Eastern meditation."

Due to the above line of research, it is my recommendation that both the clergy and laity in Christian denominations revive the early Christian practice of reading the psalms and meditating on words in the psalms. We have presented sufficient evidence that such meditation or mindfulness will tend to calm down your brain and bring a sense of peace to your life in a stressful and dangerous world. If you find yourself having fears of not being "liked" or "loved" and doubts about whether others really care about you, such praying may be especially beneficial. For the rest of us, it will center us on who we are and where we are going—to unify with God, as suggested by Teilhard de Chardin (1955).

Chardin was a Jesuit priest and anthropologist who saw evolution progressing in the future as layers of consciousness converging at the Omega Point, a supreme consciousness (God). From a personal point of view, we are all ordained to unify with God. So praying the psalms has been and can be the means to this end. In an appendix to this book, we will pick psalms used in the *Christian Prayer* (1976) that seem appropriate with key words to be used as mantras in meditating the psalms.

10

Alternate Ways to Calm the Brain

It seems important at this point to put together information on how to practice calming of your brain. To do so, returning to the research of Benson (2010) as our guide, seems appropriate.

Aerobic Exercise

What Benson found out was that aerobic exercises were just another way to elicit the relaxation response. Not everyone will be inclined to use meditation or mindfulness but still find themselves stressed and anxious at some points in the day. If you stay anxious and tense, cortisol levels will remain high and all kinds of health problems are more likely, as well as forgetfulness due to cell destruction in the hippocampus, as explained earlier. Our recommendation is about thirty minutes of continuous movement such as in running, swimming, bicycle riding, aerobic dancing, etc.

For most of my life, I have been quite active in sports of all kinds or deliberate exercises such as running, swimming, and now bicycle riding. I have found out that if I combine meditation with physical exercise, I am more able to calm myself down on demand. When I ran for many years, I would say *Jesus* to myself on one stride and *loves me* on the next stride. Now I ride a bicycle about ten miles a day and do the same thing on the downward stroke of each pedal. In so doing, the effort of running and riding was no longer attended to, and I often found myself in an extremely calm state of mind with little or no awareness of time and place. If a religious mantra does not suit your belief system, try numbers like *one* and *two* on your stride or stroke. I know other people who use the words *peace* and *calm* as they run or bike.

Occasionally using physical exercise when in a stressed state does not work very well. You need to make a life change so that the exercise is done at least three days a week for about thirty minutes each day. Your body and brain have to remain in a calm state so that when stressors arise, you can quickly and automatically return to a peaceful state of being. You have to be able to quickly center yourself and let go of future or past stressful ideas or percepts.

Repetitive Prayer

Benson's (2010) research has indicated that the relaxation response can also be elicited through repetition of prayers as indicated earlier. He suggests that the content of the prayer may not be as important as the belief behind it. If so, perhaps the repetition of Latin prayers in the mass prior to Vatican II did make Catholics feel calmer after Sunday mass and readier to take on the stresses of the week ahead. Our suggestion is that believers come to daily or weekly services in the belief that the church building is where God dwells, whether the Ark of the Covenant or the Eucharistic presence. Almost every religious tradition has its own set of prayers or devotions. The Our Father is, in the Christian tradition, such a prayer.

In attending services, it may not be as important that the believer attends to every word said but rather the experience of being in God's house, in the presence of an all-powerful God who cares about each hair on our heads (Matt. 10:30). The experience of knowing that we are safe and cared for is what calms the brain and readies us for future stressors of life. The ideal, of course, is to pray, day and night, through the use of the Divine Office or *Christian Prayer* (1976). To get the maximum effect of this continuous prayer, spread it throughout the day as intended. Because the Divine Office is repetitive, attention to the content is not as important as the experience of being in the presence of God through the repetition of the words of God.

For some, it is the repetition of a favorite prayer such as Psalm 23: "Yahweh is my Shepherd, I lack nothing…my home, the house of Yahweh, as long as I live." If you find this psalm comforting, read the psalm and imagine you are in the temple, cathedral, or among God's creation in a private place. Focus on the experience that you are in the presence of God, who loves and cares for you. We recommend that you do this for about fifteen minutes in the morning, around noon, and again in the evening. Remember that what is most important is your faith and belief that an all-powerful God cares for you and will always take care of you.

Many of the anxieties of life are about survival: having enough money to make mortgage payments, food on the table, and good friends to care for you. It is our attachment connections that allow us to feel safe and secure. Many of our problems in life are related to trusting that our needs will be met through our social attachments. If we truly believe that we are connected to a church in the widest sense, we will find comfort in those around us. The insecurely attached cannot trust that others will care for them in crisis and so live very isolated lives, attempting to fill the void with external stimulations and addictions. They, above all, need to trust in God and learn to find his presence consoling and safe.

Music

As mentioned earlier, the research at the Benson Institute (Benson and Proctor 2010) has found that playing or listening to music can also elicit the relaxation response. Music seems to be one of the primary methods used by people to regulate stress. When people are happy, they sing; and when they are sad, they sing. And yes, when bored, they whistle and sing. You also see this across the life span from children to old age. So it is not surprising to find that music helps us regulate moods. If we look at the insecurely attached, you might notice that they are angry and depressed and more inclined to get drunk or act out sexually rather than calming themselves down through pleasant music. Teenagers for many years play music at very high volume, as if to drown out the fears and anxieties of life. When the frontal lobe of the brain is more mature in the midtwenties, this trend reverses itself.

The psalms were literature developed to be accompanied by music. The psalter (the collections of 150 psalms) comes from the Greek word *psalterion*, which is the stringed instrument used for accompaniment of the psalms (The Jerusalem Bible 1966). Many of the psalms actually have musical or liturgical directions. Jewish cantors existed even in David's time. The psalter was the hymnbook of the temple and so was adopted by the early Christian Church. In summary, the psalms were made to be sung. The Jewish form of the chanting of the psalms was eventually replaced with the Gregorian chanting in the early Christian Church. Unfortunately, this great calming prayer of the church has been relegated to monasteries and seminaries where one can still witness the church in prayer.

Although one might visit monasteries or purchase CDs or records of the psalms being chanted, our recommendation is to find a quiet place and sit down in an erect position and sing the psalms in Gregorian chant, focusing on the presence of God rather than the words. The ideal is to find a group of like-minded believers who daily meet to sing the psalms together as found in the *Christian Prayer* (1976). "For where two or three meet in my name, I shall be there with them" (Matt. 18:20). This brings us back to what we said earlier about the mystical body. It is the experience of this overwhelming presence of Christ in one another that keep religious men and women dedicated to this way of life against the pressures and draw of a more materialistic world. And this appears to be the motivation of the Desert Fathers. We need to go back to their style of meditation and prayer as one means of calming the brain and having healthy, productive lives amid the complexities of the world we live in. May you and anyone with whom you have a synaptic connection have a more peaceful life because you read this book.

References

Ainsworth. M. D., Blehar, M. C., Walters, E., and Wall, S. 1978. *Patterns of Attachment: A Psychological Study of the Strange Situation.* Hillsdale, NJ: Lawrence Earlbaum Associates.

Barkley, R. A. 2012. *Executive Functions: What They Are, How They Work, and Why They Evolved.* New York: Guilford Press.

Beischel, M. L. 2010. *Attachment Tales Resolved: A Primer for Parents, Teachers, and Therapists.* Bloomington, IN: Xlibris Corporation.

———. 2012. *Case Studies on Attachment.* Second edition. Gary Way, NY: Linus Publications.

Benson, H., and Proctor, W. 2010. *Relaxation Revolution: Enhancing Your Personal Health Through the Science and Genetics of Mind Body Healing.* New York: Scribner.

Blum, D. 2002. *Love at Goon Park.* Cambridge: Perseus.

Bourne, E. J. 1995. *The Anxiety and Phobia Workbook.* Oakland, CA: New Harbinger Publications.

Bowlby, J. (1969) 1982. *Attachment and Loss: Attachment.* New York: Basic Books.

———. 1973. *Attachment and Loss, Vol. II: Separation, Anxiety, and Anger.* London: Hogarth.

Boyce, B. 2014. "No Blueprint, Just Love." *Mindful* (February 2014): 34–41.

Bamburger, J. E. 1981. Foreword to *The Abbey Psalter: The Book of Psalms Used by the Trappist Monks of Genesee Abbey* by Genessee Eudes, Eudes Bamberger, and John Abbot. New York: Paulist Press.

Cline, F. W. 1979. *Understanding and Treating the Difficult Child.* Evergreen, CO: Evergreen Consultants in Human Behavior.

Clynes, M., ed. 1982. *Music, Mind and Brain.* New York, NY: Plenum Press.

Cozolino, L. 2006. *The Neuroscience of Human Relationships Attachment and the Developing Social Brain.* New York: W.W. Norton & Company.

———. 2010. *The Neuroscience of Psychotherapy: Healing the Social Brain.* Second edition. New York: W. W. Norton & Company.

Craske, M. C., and Barlow, D. H. 2008. "Panic Disorder and Agoraphobia." In *Clinical Handbook of Psychological Disorders: A Step-by-Step Treatment Manual*, edited by D. H. Barlow. New York: Guilford Press.

Cunningham, L. S. and Egan, K. J. 1996. *Christian Spirituality: Themes from the Tradition.* Mahwah, NJ: Paulist Press.

Diederich, N. J., and Goetz, C. G. 2008. "The Placebo Treatments in Neurosciences: New Insights from Clinical Neuroimaging Studies." *Neurology* 71 (9): 677–684.

Egan, H. D. 1991. *An Anthology of Christian Mysticism*, Collegeville, MN: Liturgical Press

Ellison, C. G., and McFarland, M. J. 2013. "The Social Context of Religion and Spirituality in the Unites States." In *APA Handbook of Psychology, Religion, and Spirituality*, edited by K. I. Pargament, J. J. Exline, and J. W. Jones. Washington, DC: American Psychological Association.

Everly, G. S. and Lating, J. M. 2002. *A Clinical Guide to the Treatment of Human Stress Response*, 2nd edition. New York: Kluwer Academic/Plenum Publishing.

Filskov, S. B., Grimm, B. H., and Lewis, J. A. 1981. "Brain-Behavior Relationships." In *Handbook of Clinical Neuropsychology*, edited by S. Filskov and T. Bell. New York: Wiley & Sons.

Granqvist, P. & Kirkpatrick, L. A. (2008). Attachment and religious representations and behavior. In *Handbook of Attachment Theory, Research, and Clinical Applications*, edited by J. Cassidy and P. R. Shaver, 2nd Ed. New York: Guilford Press.

Hadot, P. and Davidson, A. I. 1995. *Philosophy as a Way of Life: Spiritual Exercise from Socrates to Foucault.* New York: Blackwell Publishing.

Hermann, D. & Macloud, E. 2007. *Helen Keller: A Determined Life.* Tonawanda, NY; Kids Can Press.

Jensen, E. (2000). *Brain–based Learning The New Science of Teaching and Training (Revised Ed.)*. Thousand Oaks, CA: Corwin Press.

Jensen, E. (2008) *Brain-based Learning The New Paradigm of Teaching, 2nd Ed*. Thousand Oaks, CA: Corwin Press.

Jha, A. P. 2013. Being in the Now. *Scientific American Mind,* March/April, 2013, 26-33.

Kavanaugh, K. & Rodriguez, O. 1991. *The Collected Works of St. John of the Cross (Revised Ed.).* Washington, D.C.: ICS Publications.

Hart, S. 2011. *The Impact of Attachment Developmental Neuroaffective Psychology*. NewYork: W W Norton & Company.

Kramer, G. W. 1992. A psychological Theory of Attachment. *Behavioral and Brain Sciences*, 15, 493-541.

Kubat-Zinn, J. 1994. *Wherever You Go, There You Are: Mindfulness Meditation in Everyday Life*. New York: Hyperion.

Lewis, D. O., Mallouh, C. and Webb, V. 1989. "Child Abuse, Delinquency, and Violent Criminality." In *Child Maltreatment Theory and Research on the Causes and Consequences of Child Abuse and Neglect,* edited by D. Cicchetti and V. Carlson. (pp.707-721). New York: Cambridge University Press.

Lu, S. 2014. How Chronic Stress is Harming our DNA. *Monitor on Psychology, 45 (No. 9), 28-31.*

Luria A. R. 1969. "Frontal lobe syndromes." In *Handbook of Clinical Neurology)*, edited by P. J. Vicken and G. Bruyn, Vol. II. Amsterdam: North Holland Publishing Co.

McCullough, M. E. and Carter, E. C. 2013. Religion, Self-control, and Self-regulation: How and Why are They Related. In K. I. Pargament, *APA Handbook of Psychology, Religion and Spirituality,* edited by K. J. Pargament, J. J. Exline and J. W. Jones. Washington, D.C.: American Psychological Association.

Merton, T. *1969. Contemplative Prayer.* New York: Image Books.

Newberg, A. and Waldman, *M. R, 2010. How God Changes Your Brain Breakthrough Findings from a Leading Nneuroscientist.* New York: Ballantine Books.

Nietzsche, F. 1883-1885. *Also Sprach Zarathustra: Ein Buch fur Alle und Keinen.* Germany: Ernst Schmeitzner.

Ogden, P. 2009. Emotion, "Mindfulness and Movement" *The Healing Power of Emotion Affective Neuroscience, Development and Clinical Practice, edited by D. Fosha, D. J. Siegel and M. F. Solomon.* NY: W. W. Norton & Company.

Congregation of the Faith, 1989. *Orationis Formas.* Retrieved from http://www.ratzinger.us/modules.php?name=News &file=article&sid=61

Papalia, D. E., Olds, S. W. and Feldman, R. D. 2004. *Human Development, 9th ed.* Boston, MA: McGraw Hill.

Pribram, K. H. (1997). "The work in Working Memory: Implications for Development." *Development of the*

Prefrontal Cortex, edited by N. A. Krasnegor, G. R. Lyon and p. S. Goldman-Rakie. Baltimore, MD: Brookes Publishing.

Schore, A. N. 2003. *Affect Dysregulation and Disorders of the Self.* New York: W. W. Norton & Company.

Segal Z. V., Williams, J. M. and Teasdale, J. D. 2002. *Mindfulness-based Cognitive Therapy for Depression A new Approach to Preventing Relapse. New York*: The Guilford Press

Shapiro. S. L. & Carlson, L. E. 2009. *The Art and Science of Mindfulness Integrating Mindfulness into Psychology and the Helping Professions.* Washington, D.C.: American Psychological Association.

Shults, F. L. 2002. The "Body of Christ" in evangelical theology. *Word and World.* 22, no. 2, 178-185

"6 ways to shrink-proof your brain." 2015. *Mind, Mood & Memory. Vol 11, No. 10. Norwalk. CT: Massachusetts General Hospital.*

Somer, E. 1999, *Food and Mood, the Complete Guide to Eating Well and Feeling Your Best.* New York: Henry Holt and Company.

Sroufe, L. A., Egeland, B. and Kreutzer, T. 1990. "The Fate of Early Experience following Developmental Change. *Child Development*, 61, 1363-1373.

The New Jerusalem Bible. 1998. Standard Edition. New York: Doubleday.

Teasdale, J., Williams, M. and Segal, Z, 2014. *The Mindful Way Workbook An 8-week Program to Free Yourself from Depression and Emotional Distress*. New York: The Guilford Press.

Teilhard de Chardin, P. *1955. The Phenomenon of Man*. New York: Harper and Rowe.

Von Balthasar, H. U. 1989. *Christian Meditation*. San Francisco, CA: Ignatius Press.

Weinberger, N. 1995. "Nonmusical Outcomes of Music Education." *Musical Journal*. Fall: II(2):6.

Wortley, J. 2006. "How the Desert Fathers 'Meditated.'" *Greek, Roman and Byzantine Studies*. 46:315-328. Retrieved Febrary 11, 2015 from http://www.duke.edu/classics/grbs/Ftexts/...wortley.pdf.

Zukerman, P. 2005. "Atheism: Contemporary Rates and Patterns." In *The Cambridge Companion to Atheism*, edited by M. Martin. Cambridge, England: Cambridge University Press.

Appendix

Selected Psalms and Focus Words

HERE ARE SOME PSALMS SELECTED from the *Christian Prayer: The Liturgy of the Hours* (1976) with commentary and focus words to use in Christian meditation. We have not followed the exact formatting and verse numbers found in the New Jerusalem Bible (1998) in presenting the psalms.

Psalm 5

This is a morning prayer attributed to David appropriate to anyone who feels persecuted ("Not a word from their lips can be trusted"). It is the prayer for anyone who trusts that when everyone else is against you, God will protect you. This is certainly the feeling of the insecurely attached, as well as anyone who is hit with many stressors at once, and especially if you feel deceived by a "loved one."

Give ear to my words, Yahweh, spare a thought for my
   sighing.
Listen to my cry for help, my King and my God!
To you I pray, Yahweh.
At daybreak you hear my voice; at daybreak I lay my case
   before you and fix my eyes on you.
You are not a God who takes pleasure in evil, no sinner can
   be your guest.
Boasters cannot stand their ground under your gaze.
You hate evil-doers, liars you destroy; the violent and
   deceitful
Yahweh detests
But, so great is your faithful love, I may come into your
   house, and before your holy temple bow down in
   reverence of you.
In your saving justice, Yahweh lead me, because of those
   who lie in wait for me; make you way plain before me.
Not a word from their lips can be trusted, through and
   through they are destruction, their throats are wide-
   open graves, their tongues destructive.
Lay the guilt on them, God, make their intrigues their
   own downfall; for their own countless offences, thrust
   them from you, since they have rebelled against you,
   those who love your name.
It is you who bless the upright, Yahweh, you surround
   them with favor as with a shield. (Ps. 5:1–12, NJB)

Now get into a meditative posture as described earlier and
repeat the focus phrase "faithful love." Based on the work

of Benson, it is appropriate to generate an image of God perhaps protecting you with a shield. Continue to repeat the focus words. If other thoughts enter your mind, just return to the focus words without any sense of judgment.

Psalm 24

This is another Davidic morning prayer. It asks the question about who is ready to be in the presence of God. The answer is the "clean of hands and pure of heart." This is a great prayer for those who find themselves weak and stuck on the "vanities" of the world. This psalm is a great prayer for anyone with weaknesses, such as addictions. To dare be in the presence of God, we have to leave behind those temptations and cling to God, the "King of Glory."

> To Yahweh belong the earth and all it contains, the world and all who live there;
> It is he who laid its foundations on the seas, on the flowing waters fixed it firm.
> Who shall go up to the mountain of Yahweh?
> Who shall take a stand in his holy place?
> The clean of hands and pure of heart, whose heart is not set on vanities,
> Who does not swear an oath in order to deceive.
> Such a one will receive blessings from Yahweh, saving justice from the God of his salvation.
> Such is the people that seeks him, that seeks your presence, God of Jacob.

Gates, lift high your heads, raise high the ancient gateways,
And the king of glory shall enter!
Who is he, this king of glory?
Yahweh Sabaoth, he is the king of glory. (Ps. 24, NJB)

After reading this psalm, use the focus words "King of glory." Repeat that phrase over and over, focusing your attention on those words. Perhaps generate an image of the King of Glory coming, such as Christ's arrival in Jerusalem with crowds honoring Him with the waving of palms. Let go of all anxieties in the future and be absorbed in the present moment of Christ's glory. You don't have to be anywhere or be anything. You just have to be in the presence of Christ.

Psalm 36

This is another Davidic psalm that compares the sinner who feels no guilt or fear of God to the faithful who takes refuge under God's wings, where they will be cared for due to God's faithful love. For the insecurely attached, this protection for food and survival is cherished. And the protection will continue because God's love is faithful. On the other hand, the wicked evildoers will fail, and God will protect us from them. This is also a great prayer for Americans who have been taught to develop self-care to the exclusion of caring for others. We survive by turning to others and helping one another through the body of Christ. The more trauma and danger we see in our world, the more we need the attitude of turning to God for protection.

> Sin is the oracle of the wicked in the depths of his heart; there is no fear of God before his eyes.
>
> He sees himself with too flattering an eye to detect and detest his guilt; all he says is malicious and deceitful, he has turned his back on wisdom.
>
> To get his way he hatches malicious plots, even in his bed; once set on his evil course no wickedness is too much for him.
>
> Yahweh, your faithful love is in the heavens, your constancy reaches to the clouds, your saving justice is like towering mountains, your judgments like the mighty deep.
>
> Yahweh, you support both man and beast; how precious, God, is your faithful love.
>
> So the children of Adam take refuge in the shadow of your wings.
>
> They feast on the bounty of your house, you let them drink from your delicious streams; in you is the source of life, by your light we see the light.
>
> Maintain your faithful love to those who acknowledge you, and your saving justice to the honest of heart.
>
> Do not let the foot of the arrogant overtake me or wicked hands drive me away. there they have fallen, the evil-doers, flung down, never to rise again. (Ps. 36, NJB)

The focus phrase for this psalm is "in the shadow of your wings." Repeat this phrase over and over while feeling the peace of being under the protection of God's loving wings. Let no words or images distract you from this sense of peace and quiet.

Psalm 51

This psalm has been attributed to David after Nathan told him that he would lose an offspring due to killing Uriah and taking the latter's wife, Bathsheba. It is a story of a man abusing his power and sinning and then repenting. Nathan makes it clear that Yahweh forgives David.

So this psalm is the prayer of repentance of a man who believes and trusts in God's protection and forgiveness. This is a very good prayer for someone who sins addictively and keeps returning to God for forgiveness. It is the prayer of someone who sins out of selfishness but realizes later how he has turned away from God.

> Have mercy on me, O God, in your faithful love, in your great tenderness wipe away my offenses; wash me clean from my guilt, purify me from my sin.
> For I am well aware of my offenses, my sin is constantly in my mind.
> Against you, you alone, I have sinned, I have done what you see to be wrong, that you may show your saving justice when you pass sentence, and your victory may appear when you give judgment, remember, I was born guilty, a sinner from the moment of conception.

But you delight in sincerity of heart, and in secret you teach me wisdom.

Purify me with hyssop till I am clean, wash me until I am whiter than snow.

Let me hear the sound of joy and gladness, and the bones you have crushed will dance.

Turn away your face from my sins, and wipe away all my guilt.

God, create in me a clean heart, renew within me a resolute spirit, do not thrust me away from your presence, do not take away from me your spirit of holiness.

Give me back the joy of your salvation, sustain in me a generous spirit.

I shall teach the wicked your paths, and sinners will return to you.

Deliver me from bloodshed, God, God of my salvation, and my tongue will acclaim your saving justice.

Lord, open my lips, and my mouth will speak out your praise.

Sacrifice gives you no pleasure, burnt offering you do not desire.

Sacrifice to God is a broken spirit, a broken, contrite heart you never scorn.

In your graciousness do good to Zion, rebuild the walls of Jerusalem.

Then you will delight in upright sacrifices,—burnt offerings and whole oblations—and young bulls will be offered on your altar. (Ps. 51, NJB)

A good stimulus word to repeat in meditating is "Have mercy on me, O God." This allows one to take the position of one who has turned away from the presence of God through selfishness. A possible image to focus on is yourself being washed unlit, "whiter than snow." We now turn back knowing how much we need to be absorbed in his presence. We are now fit to be in his presence.

Psalm 57

In the biblical book of 1 Samuel, we are told the story of King Saul disobeying Yahweh and falling out of His favor and the story of David killing Goliath with the power given by Yahweh. Saul is then pictured as wanting to kill David out of jealousy. David then goes into hiding in caves and mountains to avoid being killed by Saul. David has Yahweh's protection through all of this. Psalm 57 is perhaps the prayer of David fearing for his life. What a wonderful prayer for the insecurely attached who live at a survival level, always trying to control others lest they perish. This is a wonderful prayer for anyone who is up against a powerful enemy: criminals on the run, children who are being bullied, employees who feel that they are not valued, and perhaps all adolescents who are trying to assert their own identity at the time.

> Take pity on me, God, take pity on me, for in you I take refuge,
> In the shadow of your wings I take refuge, until the destruction is past.

I call to God the most high, to God who has done everything for me; may he send from heaven and save me; and check those who harry me; may God send his faithful love and his constancy.

I lie surrounded by lions, greedy for human prey, their teeth are spears and arrows, their tongue a sharp sword.

Be exalted above the heavens, God! Your glory over all the earth!

They laid a snare in my path—I was bowed with care—they dug a pit ahead of me, but fell in it themselves.

My heart is ready, God, my heart is ready;

I will sing, and make music for you.

Awake, my glory, awake, lyre and harp, that I may awake the Dawn.

I will praise you among the peoples, Lord, I will make music for you among nations, for your faithful love towers to heaven, your constancy to the clouds.

Be exalted above the heavens, God!

Your glory over all the earth! (Ps. 57, NJB)

Although there are many meaningful phrases in this psalm, I would suggest that the focus phrase be "In you I take refuge." The image that I recommend is from the psalm—surrounded by lions exposing their sharp teeth, you are whisked away by a large bird that tucks you under her wings and flies you out of danger. It is interesting to note that David accompanies his praise of God with music. Given what we have learned form Benson and others, an alternate image is visualizing David playing his harp under the protection of God.

Psalm 121

This is a psalm sung by pilgrims as they made their way up to Jerusalem. This psalm pictures the psalmist faced with traversing a mountain range and wondering if they can make it over the mountain. The entreaty or prayer is that Yahweh, who made heaven and earth, can certainly help them, lest they slip. They will be protected both day and night "from all harm." This is a wonderful prayer for anyone facing difficult tasks or obstacles in life. For those stuck in survival fears, it is especially meaningful. Many people worry about being successful in life's endeavors. Trusting that God will protect us day and night (when we have to let our guard down to go asleep) enables us to be at peace as we go about our daily routines.

> I lift up my eyes to the mountains; where is my help to come from?
> My help comes from Yahweh who made heaven and earth.
> May he save your foot from stumbling; may he, your guardian, not fall asleep!
> You see—he neither sleeps nor slumbers, the guardian of Israel.
> Yahweh is your guardian, your shade, Yahweh, at your right hand.
> By day the sun will not strike you, nor the moon by night.
> Yahweh guards you from all harm
> Yahweh guards your life,

Yahweh guards your comings and goings, henceforth and
for ever. (Ps. 121, NJB)

The recommended focus word in this short psalm is
"My help comes from Yahweh." You might picture yourself
trudging up a steep mountainside, fearing that you might
slip but trusting with each step that God will protect you
from falling.

Psalm 142

This is another prayer attributed to David as he hid from Saul,
fearing for his life. This is clearly the entreaty of someone
who is in survival mode. No one is there to help him, and
apparently no one dares to help him. He clearly expresses the
fear of abandonment. The picture is of one who is tired and
weak from trying to avoid death. As weak and abandoned
as he feels, David still trusts that Yahweh will rescue him.
He places himself in the presence of Yahweh to "unfold
my troubles."

What a wonderful prayer for the insecurely attached who
feels abandoned and unloved. Even if everyone else abandons
them, God will not. This also is a great prayer for people
with health problems who are feeling weak and lonely, trying
to accept their illness and final fear of death. This is also a
great prayer for those with addictions who feel helpless and
weak in controlling the addiction—imprisoned by their own
repetitive behavior.

To Yahweh I cry out with my plea.

To Yahweh I cry out with entreaty.

I pour out my worry in his presence, in his presence I unfold my troubles.

However faint my spirit; you are watching over my path.

On the road I have to travel they have hidden trap for me.

Look on my right and see—there is no one who recognises me.

All refuge is denied me, no one cares whether I live or die.

I cry out to you, Yahweh, I affirm "You are my refuge, my share in the land of the living!"

Listen to my calling, for I am miserably weak.

Rescue me from my persecutors, for they are too strong for me.

Lead me out of prison that I may praise your name.

The upright gather round me because of your generosity to me. (Ps. 142, NJB)

The focus word that I recommend is "To Yahweh I cry out." A visualization that might be used is the sight of Christ coming to pick you up in your sickness, abandonment, or addiction and caring for you in your weakness.